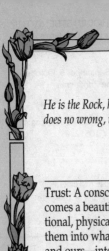

He is the Rock, his works are perfect, and all his ways are just. A faith[ful God] does no wrong, upright and just is he.

Deutero[nomy]

Trust: A conscious act of placing each child in his hands. With tha[t] comes a beautiful awareness that through each experience—socia[l, emo]tional, physical, and intellectual—he is at work in their lives. He i[s shaping] them into what he would have them become. He is turning their f[ootsteps—] and ours—into footsteps . . . footsteps toward himself.

Dia[ne]

PASSAGE FOR THE DAY:
Deuteronomy 32:1–4

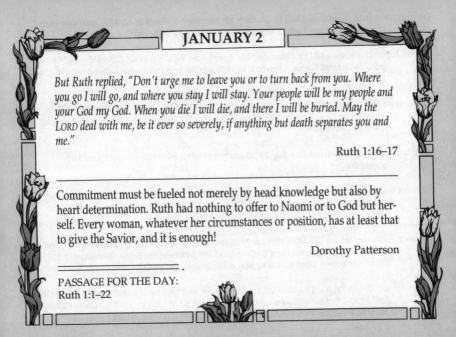

But Ruth replied, "Don't urge me to leave you or to turn back from you. Where you go I will go, and where you stay I will stay. Your people will be my people and your God my God. When you die I will die, and there I will be buried. May the LORD deal with me, be it ever so severely, if anything but death separates you and me."

Ruth 1:16–17

Commitment must be fueled not merely by head knowledge but also by heart determination. Ruth had nothing to offer to Naomi or to God but herself. Every woman, whatever her circumstances or position, has at least that to give the Savior, and it is enough!

Dorothy Patterson

PASSAGE FOR THE DAY:
Ruth 1:1–22

JANUARY 3

But now, this is why the LORD says—he who created you, O Jacob, he who formed you, O Israel: "Fear not, for I have redeemed you; I have summoned you by name; you are mine. When you pass through the waters, I will be with you; and when you pass through the rivers, they will not sweep over you. When you walk through the fire, you will not be burned; the flames will not set you ablaze. For I am the LORD, your God, the Holy One of Israel, your Savior; I give Egypt for your ransom, Cush and Seba in your stead."

Isaiah 43:1–3

Can we imagine that God, who is concerned with so many stupendous things, can possibly be concerned about us? We do imagine it. We hope he is. Where else can we possibly turn when we have come to the end of our resources?

Elisabeth Elliot

PASSAGE FOR THE DAY:
Isaiah 43:1–13

Wives, in the same way be submissive to your husbands so that, if any of them do not believe the word, they may be won over without words by the behavior of their wives.

I Peter 3:1

A lovely Christian woman came to us with a troubled, broken heart. She was married to a man who had professed Jesus Christ years before, but who had turned away from those beliefs. She learned through study of the Word that submission to and love for her husband was an outgrowth of spiritual development and a close relationship with the Lord.

Beverly LaHaye

PASSAGE FOR THE DAY:
I Peter 3:1–6

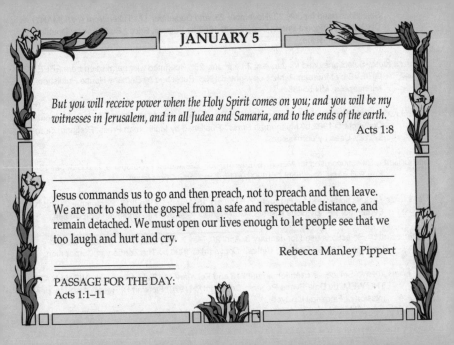

JANUARY 5

But you will receive power when the Holy Spirit comes on you; and you will be my witnesses in Jerusalem, and in all Judea and Samaria, and to the ends of the earth.

Acts 1:8

Jesus commands us to go and then preach, not to preach and then leave. We are not to shout the gospel from a safe and respectable distance, and remain detached. We must open our lives enough to let people see that we too laugh and hurt and cry.

Rebecca Manley Pippert

PASSAGE FOR THE DAY:
Acts 1:1–11

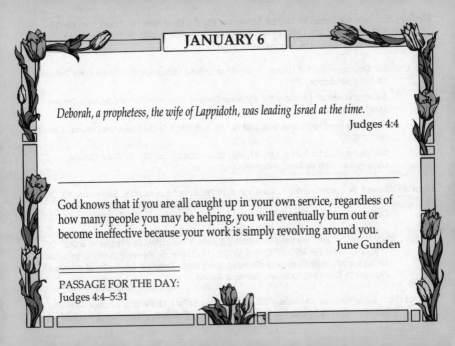

JANUARY 6

Deborah, a prophetess, the wife of Lappidoth, was leading Israel at the time.

Judges 4:4

God knows that if you are all caught up in your own service, regardless of how many people you may be helping, you will eventually burn out or become ineffective because your work is simply revolving around you.

June Gunden

PASSAGE FOR THE DAY:
Judges 4:4–5:31

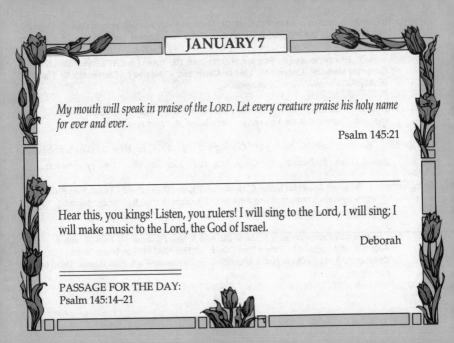

JANUARY 7

My mouth will speak in praise of the LORD. Let every creature praise his holy name for ever and ever.

Psalm 145:21

Hear this, you kings! Listen, you rulers! I will sing to the Lord, I will sing; I will make music to the Lord, the God of Israel.

Deborah

PASSAGE FOR THE DAY:
Psalm 145:14–21

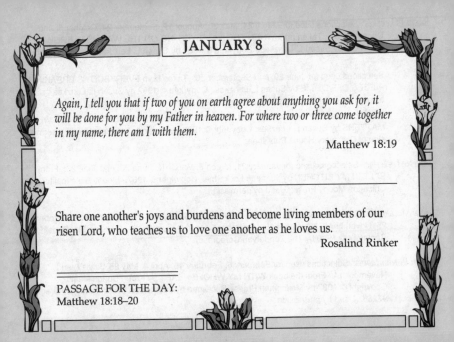

JANUARY 8

Again, I tell you that if two of you on earth agree about anything you ask for, it will be done for you by my Father in heaven. For where two or three come together in my name, there am I with them.

Matthew 18:19

Share one another's joys and burdens and become living members of our risen Lord, who teaches us to love one another as he loves us.

Rosalind Rinker

PASSAGE FOR THE DAY:
Matthew 18:18–20

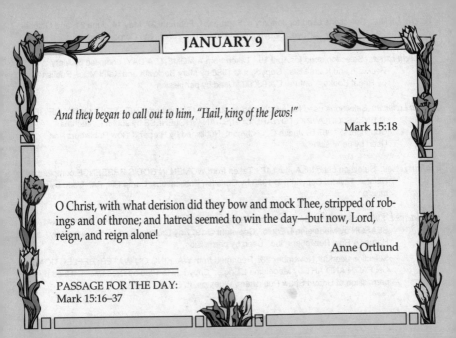

JANUARY 9

And they began to call out to him, "Hail, king of the Jews!"

Mark 15:18

O Christ, with what derision did they bow and mock Thee, stripped of robings and of throne; and hatred seemed to win the day—but now, Lord, reign, and reign alone!

Anne Ortlund

PASSAGE FOR THE DAY:
Mark 15:16–37

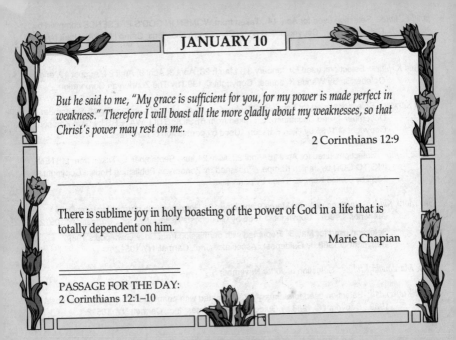

JANUARY 10

But he said to me, "My grace is sufficient for you, for my power is made perfect in weakness." Therefore I will boast all the more gladly about my weaknesses, so that Christ's power may rest on me.

2 Corinthians 12:9

There is sublime joy in holy boasting of the power of God in a life that is totally dependent on him.

Marie Chapian

PASSAGE FOR THE DAY:
2 Corinthians 12:1–10

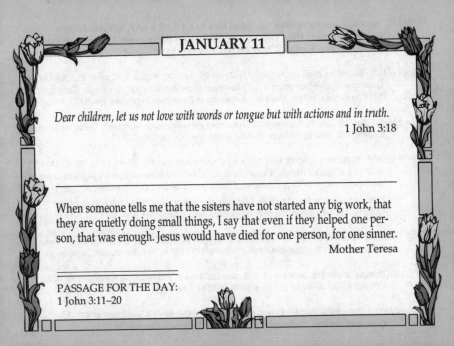

JANUARY 11

Dear children, let us not love with words or tongue but with actions and in truth.

1 John 3:18

When someone tells me that the sisters have not started any big work, that they are quietly doing small things, I say that even if they helped one person, that was enough. Jesus would have died for one person, for one sinner.

Mother Teresa

PASSAGE FOR THE DAY:
1 John 3:11–20

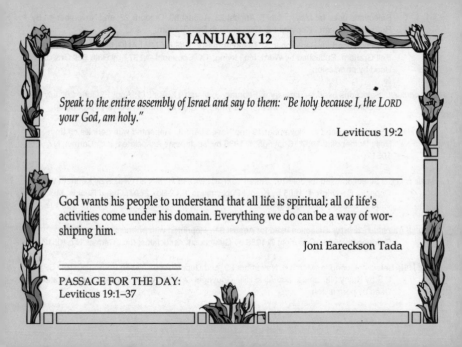

JANUARY 12

Speak to the entire assembly of Israel and say to them: "Be holy because I, the LORD your God, am holy."

Leviticus 19:2

God wants his people to understand that all life is spiritual; all of life's activities come under his domain. Everything we do can be a way of worshiping him.

Joni Eareckson Tada

PASSAGE FOR THE DAY:
Leviticus 19:1–37

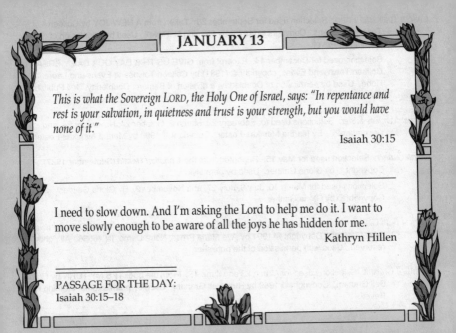

JANUARY 13

This is what the Sovereign LORD, the Holy One of Israel, says: "In repentance and rest is your salvation, in quietness and trust is your strength, but you would have none of it."

Isaiah 30:15

I need to slow down. And I'm asking the Lord to help me do it. I want to move slowly enough to be aware of all the joys he has hidden for me.

Kathryn Hillen

PASSAGE FOR THE DAY:
Isaiah 30:15–18

JANUARY 14

And when the Israelites saw the great power the LORD displayed against the Egyptians, the people feared the LORD and put their trust in him and in Moses his servant.

Exodus 14:31

We are slow to remember God's goodness, yet quick to complain. We doubt the protection and provision of our God. Perhaps we ought to take the advice God gave those Israelites in Deuteronomy 4:9: "Only be careful and watch yourselves closely so that you do not forget the things your eyes have seen."

Joni Eareckson Tada

PASSAGE FOR THE DAY:
Exodus 14:1–15:27

JANUARY 15

Is anything too hard for the LORD? I will return to you at the appointed time next year and Sarah will have a son.

Genesis 18:14

God knows how far we've progressed in our hopes and dreams. He hears our weeping. Don't mess up your life with do-it-yourself projects when God has promised the very best for you.

Gladys M. Hunt

PASSAGE FOR THE DAY:
Genesis 16:1–16 and 18:1–15

JANUARY 16

I will give you a new heart and put a new spirit in you; I will remove from you your heart of stone and give you a heart of flesh.

Ezekiel 36:26

Every person needs a new heart. In a spiritual sense, God takes your "diseased" heart and replaces it with a new one. Slowly, after this divine transplant, healing begins; and as promised, your new heart becomes capable of perfect love.

June Hunt

PASSAGE FOR THE DAY:
Ezekiel 36:13–32

ACKNOWLEDGMENTS

Myrna Alexander: Selections used for April 1, April 21, July 3, and September 9. Taken from WITH HIM IN THE STRUGGLE: A WOMAN'S WORKSHOP ON II SAMUEL Copyright © 1992 by Myrna Alexander. Used by permission.

Ann Kiemel Anderson: Selections used for August 8, September 18, and November 18. By Ann Kiemel Anderson. Copyright © 1990 by The Zondervan Corporation.

Gini Andrews: Selections used for May 17, July 1, August 27, September 14, October 4, and December 7. Taken from A VIOLENT GRACE by Gini Andrews. Copyright © 1986 by Gini Andrews. Used by permission of Zondervan Publishing House.

Carol L. Baldwin: Selections used for January 17, May 19, June 13, August 4, August 6, September 29, November 10, November 27, December 6, and December 20. By Carol L. Baldwin. Copyright © 1990 by The Zondervan Corporation.

Alma Barkman: Selections used for February 16 and July 7. From RISE AND SHINE by Alma Barkman. Copyright © 1987. Moody Bible Institute of Chicago. Moody Press. Used by permission.

Selections used for September 13 and October 2. From SUNNY-SIDE UP by Alma Barkman. Copyright © 1977. Moody Bible Institute of Chicago. Moody Press. Used by permission.

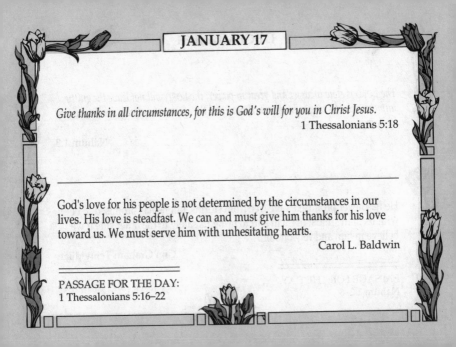

JANUARY 17

Give thanks in all circumstances, for this is God's will for you in Christ Jesus.

1 Thessalonians 5:18

God's love for his people is not determined by the circumstances in our lives. His love is steadfast. We can and must give him thanks for his love toward us. We must serve him with unhesitating hearts.

Carol L. Baldwin

PASSAGE FOR THE DAY:
1 Thessalonians 5:16–22

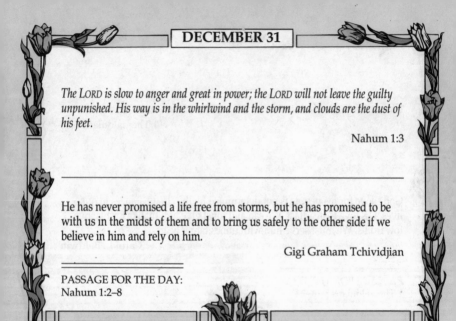

DECEMBER 31

The LORD is slow to anger and great in power; the LORD will not leave the guilty unpunished. His way is in the whirlwind and the storm, and clouds are the dust of his feet.

Nahum 1:3

He has never promised a life free from storms, but he has promised to be with us in the midst of them and to bring us safely to the other side if we believe in him and rely on him.

Gigi Graham Tchividjian

PASSAGE FOR THE DAY:
Nahum 1:2–8

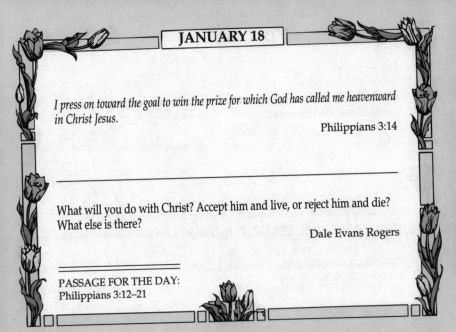

I press on toward the goal to win the prize for which God has called me heavenward in Christ Jesus.

Philippians 3:14

What will you do with Christ? Accept him and live, or reject him and die? What else is there?

Dale Evans Rogers

PASSAGE FOR THE DAY:
Philippians 3:12–21

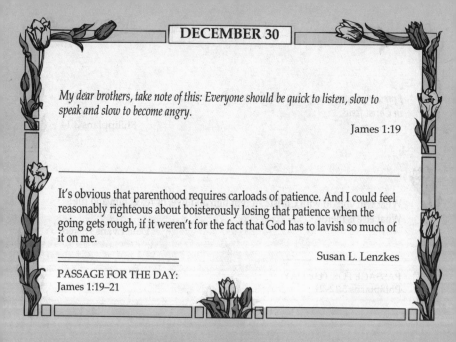

My dear brothers, take note of this: Everyone should be quick to listen, slow to speak and slow to become angry.

James 1:19

It's obvious that parenthood requires carloads of patience. And I could feel reasonably righteous about boisterously losing that patience when the going gets rough, if it weren't for the fact that God has to lavish so much of it on me.

Susan L. Lenzkes

PASSAGE FOR THE DAY:
James 1:19–21

JANUARY 19

Arise, shine, for your light has come, and the glory of the LORD rises upon you. See, darkness covers the earth and thick darkness is over the peoples, but the LORD rises upon you and his glory appears over you. Nations will come to your light, and kings to the brightness of your dawn.

Isaiah 60:1–3

Exposing ourselves to the light and presence of the Lord's love not only will uncover the dark places of our hearts but also will fill them with light. Come to God with an honest expression of willingness to allow him to change us—by his wonderful and brilliant light.

Debby Boone

PASSAGE FOR THE DAY:
Isaiah 60:1–9

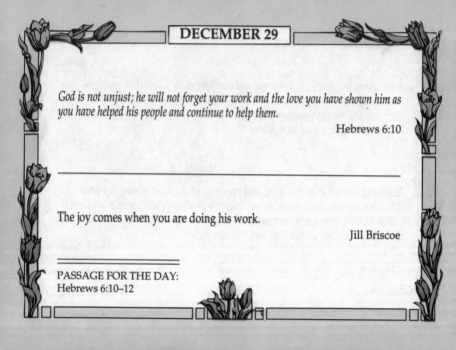

DECEMBER 29

God is not unjust; he will not forget your work and the love you have shown him as you have helped his people and continue to help them.

Hebrews 6:10

The joy comes when you are doing his work.

Jill Briscoe

PASSAGE FOR THE DAY:
Hebrews 6:10–12

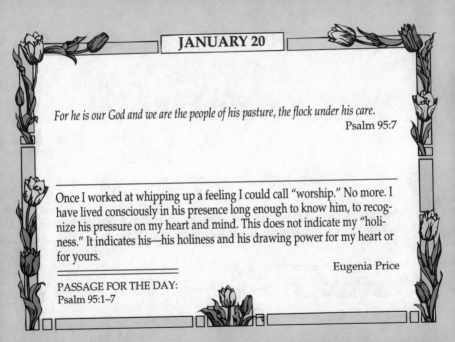

For he is our God and we are the people of his pasture, the flock under his care.

Psalm 95:7

Once I worked at whipping up a feeling I could call "worship." No more. I have lived consciously in his presence long enough to know him, to recognize his pressure on my heart and mind. This does not indicate my "holiness." It indicates his—his holiness and his drawing power for my heart or for yours.

Eugenia Price

PASSAGE FOR THE DAY:
Psalm 95:1–7

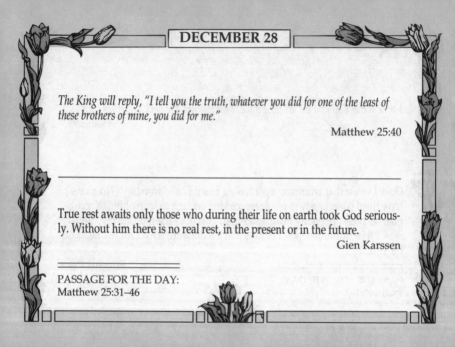

DECEMBER 28

The King will reply, "I tell you the truth, whatever you did for one of the least of these brothers of mine, you did for me."

Matthew 25:40

True rest awaits only those who during their life on earth took God seriously. Without him there is no real rest, in the present or in the future.

Gien Karssen

PASSAGE FOR THE DAY:
Matthew 25:31–46

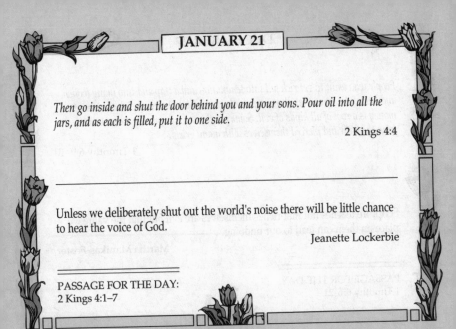

JANUARY 21

Then go inside and shut the door behind you and your sons. Pour oil into all the jars, and as each is filled, put it to one side.

2 Kings 4:4

Unless we deliberately shut out the world's noise there will be little chance to hear the voice of God.

Jeanette Lockerbie

PASSAGE FOR THE DAY:
2 Kings 4:1–7

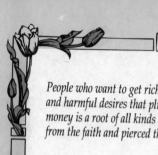

DECEMBER 27

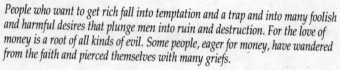

People who want to get rich fall into temptation and a trap and into many foolish and harmful desires that plunge men into ruin and destruction. For the love of money is a root of all kinds of evil. Some people, eager for money, have wandered from the faith and pierced themselves with many griefs.

1 Timothy 6:9–10

Scripture teaches not that riches themselves are evil but that the value we place on them can lead to our undoing.

Martha Manikas-Foster

PASSAGE FOR THE DAY:
1 Timothy 6:1–21

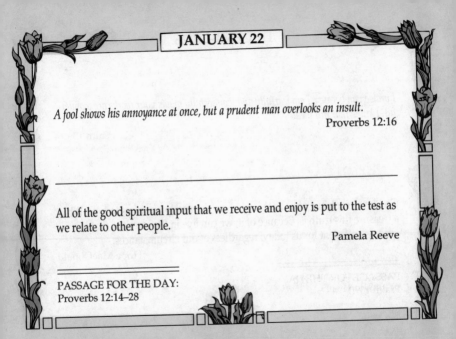

JANUARY 22

A fool shows his annoyance at once, but a prudent man overlooks an insult.

Proverbs 12:16

All of the good spiritual input that we receive and enjoy is put to the test as we relate to other people.

Pamela Reeve

PASSAGE FOR THE DAY:
Proverbs 12:14–28

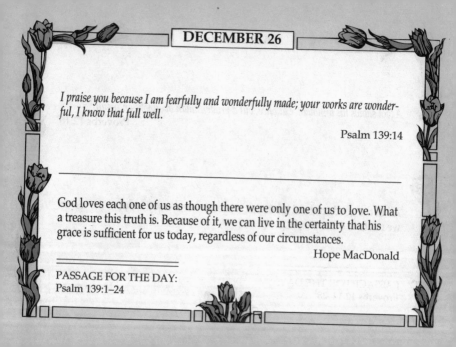

DECEMBER 26

I praise you because I am fearfully and wonderfully made; your works are wonderful, I know that full well.

Psalm 139:14

God loves each one of us as though there were only one of us to love. What a treasure this truth is. Because of it, we can live in the certainty that his grace is sufficient for us today, regardless of our circumstances.

Hope MacDonald

PASSAGE FOR THE DAY:
Psalm 139:1–24

JANUARY 23

Therefore I wail over Moab, for all Moab I cry out, I moan for the men of Kir Hareseth. Joy and gladness are gone from the orchards and fields of Moab. I have stopped the flow of wine from the presses; no one treads them with shouts of joy. Although there are shouts, they are not shouts of joy.

Jeremiah 48:31, 33

Even in the depths of sorrow, hope breathes. Hope in God's capacity to infuse suffering with purpose. And hope that because of his healing power, your sorrow will not go on forever.

Maureen Rank

PASSAGE FOR THE DAY:
Jeremiah 48:29–38

DECEMBER 25

Today in the town of David a Savior has been born to you; he is Christ the Lord.

Luke 2:11

For unto us a son was given and he was called God With Us. For those of us who believe, the whole world is decorated in love!

Ann Weems

PASSAGE FOR THE DAY:
Luke 2:1–20

JANUARY 24

He answered: "Love the Lord your God with all your heart and with all your soul and with all your strength and with all your mind"; and, "Love your neighbor as yourself."

Luke 10:27

It is easy to think of the poverty far away and forget very quickly. Today a great disease is that feeling of terrible loneliness, the feeling of being unwanted, having forgotten what human joy is, what the human feeling is of being wanted or loved.

Mother Teresa

PASSAGE FOR THE DAY:
Luke 10:25–37

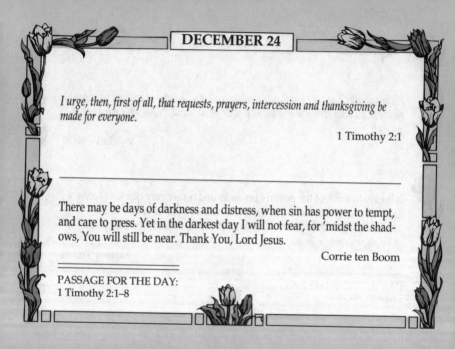

DECEMBER 24

I urge, then, first of all, that requests, prayers, intercession and thanksgiving be made for everyone.

1 Timothy 2:1

There may be days of darkness and distress, when sin has power to tempt, and care to press. Yet in the darkest day I will not fear, for 'midst the shadows, You will still be near. Thank You, Lord Jesus.

Corrie ten Boom

PASSAGE FOR THE DAY:
1 Timothy 2:1–8

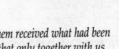

JANUARY 25

These were all commended for their faith, yet none of them received what had been promised. God had planned something better for us so that only together with us would they be made perfect.

Hebrews 11:39–40

Faith willfully chooses even disgrace or mistreatment because it sees, through an act of trust, the eventual reward that comes from him who is invisible.

Luci Swindoll

PASSAGE FOR THE DAY:
Hebrews 11:23–29, 39–40

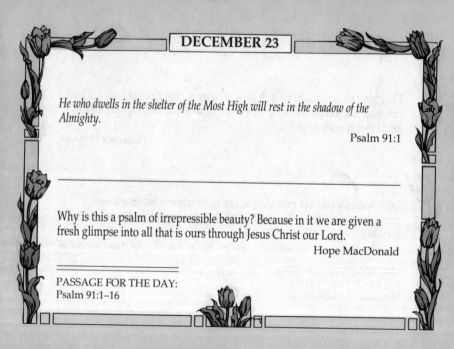

He who dwells in the shelter of the Most High will rest in the shadow of the Almighty.

Psalm 91:1

Why is this a psalm of irrepressible beauty? Because in it we are given a fresh glimpse into all that is ours through Jesus Christ our Lord.

Hope MacDonald

PASSAGE FOR THE DAY:
Psalm 91:1–16

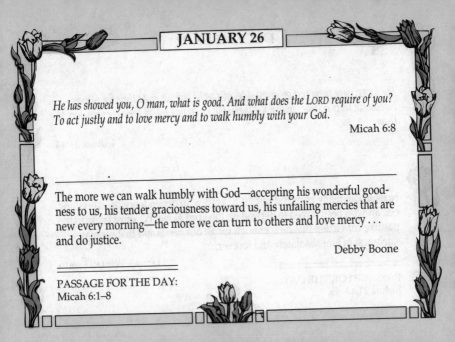

JANUARY 26

He has showed you, O man, what is good. And what does the LORD require of you? To act justly and to love mercy and to walk humbly with your God.

Micah 6:8

The more we can walk humbly with God—accepting his wonderful goodness to us, his tender graciousness toward us, his unfailing mercies that are new every morning—the more we can turn to others and love mercy . . . and do justice.

Debby Boone

PASSAGE FOR THE DAY:
Micah 6:1–8

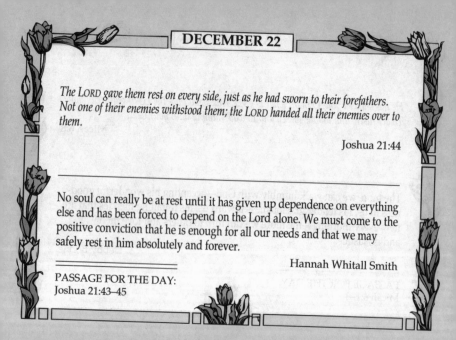

DECEMBER 22

The LORD gave them rest on every side, just as he had sworn to their forefathers. Not one of their enemies withstood them; the LORD handed all their enemies over to them.

Joshua 21:44

No soul can really be at rest until it has given up dependence on everything else and has been forced to depend on the Lord alone. We must come to the positive conviction that he is enough for all our needs and that we may safely rest in him absolutely and forever.

Hannah Whitall Smith

PASSAGE FOR THE DAY:
Joshua 21:43–45

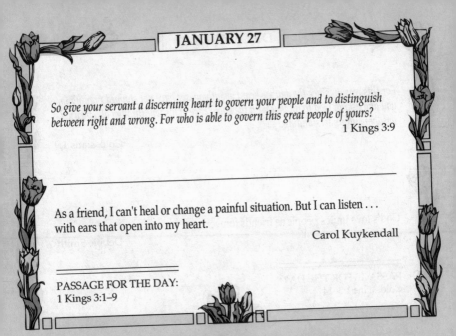

JANUARY 27

So give your servant a discerning heart to govern your people and to distinguish between right and wrong. For who is able to govern this great people of yours?

1 Kings 3:9

As a friend, I can't heal or change a painful situation. But I can listen . . . with ears that open into my heart.

Carol Kuykendall

PASSAGE FOR THE DAY:
1 Kings 3:1–9

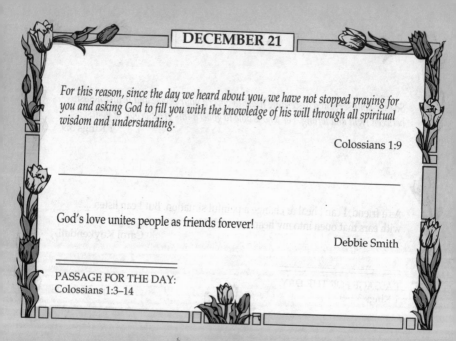

DECEMBER 21

For this reason, since the day we heard about you, we have not stopped praying for you and asking God to fill you with the knowledge of his will through all spiritual wisdom and understanding.

Colossians 1:9

God's love unites people as friends forever!

Debbie Smith

PASSAGE FOR THE DAY:
Colossians 1:3–14

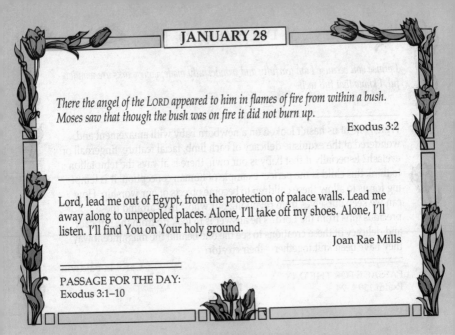

JANUARY 28

There the angel of the LORD appeared to him in flames of fire from within a bush. Moses saw that though the bush was on fire it did not burn up.

Exodus 3:2

Lord, lead me out of Egypt, from the protection of palace walls. Lead me away along to unpeopled places. Alone, I'll take off my shoes. Alone, I'll listen. I'll find You on Your holy ground.

Joan Rae Mills

PASSAGE FOR THE DAY:
Exodus 3:1–10

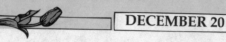

DECEMBER 20

I praise you because I am fearfully and wonderfully made; your works are wonderful, I know that full well.

Psalm 139:14

Which one of us hasn't looked on a newborn baby with amazement and wondered at the exquisite delicacy of each limb, facial feature, fingernail or eyelash? Especially if that baby is our own, there is always the temptation to think this child is the perfect example of human conception. It is tempting for us to allow these children to become objects of our worship. How can we keep ourselves from revolving our whole lives around these precious gifts from the Lord? The answer is to look up from the intricacy and delicacy of these creations to see the one behind the magnificent way they have been knit together—their creator.

Carol L. Baldwin

PASSAGE FOR THE DAY:
Psalm 139:1–24

JANUARY 29

So he went to her, took her hand and helped her up. The fever left her and she began to wait on them.

Mark 1:31

You do not need to twist arms once you have had a personal encounter with the Christ of Galilee. Ministry is not then a maybe—it's a must.

Jill Briscoe

PASSAGE FOR THE DAY:
Mark 1:29–34

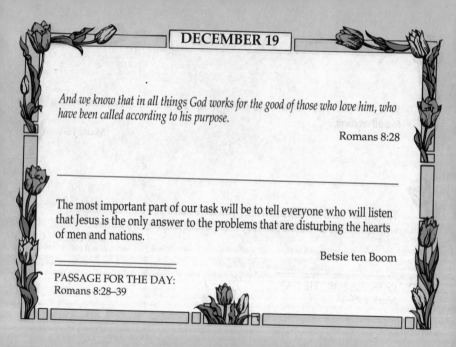

DECEMBER 19

And we know that in all things God works for the good of those who love him, who have been called according to his purpose.

Romans 8:28

The most important part of our task will be to tell everyone who will listen that Jesus is the only answer to the problems that are disturbing the hearts of men and nations.

Betsie ten Boom

PASSAGE FOR THE DAY:
Romans 8:28–39

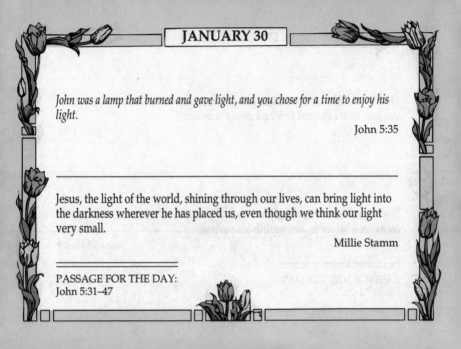

JANUARY 30

John was a lamp that burned and gave light, and you chose for a time to enjoy his light.

John 5:35

Jesus, the light of the world, shining through our lives, can bring light into the darkness wherever he has placed us, even though we think our light very small.

Millie Stamm

PASSAGE FOR THE DAY:
John 5:31–47

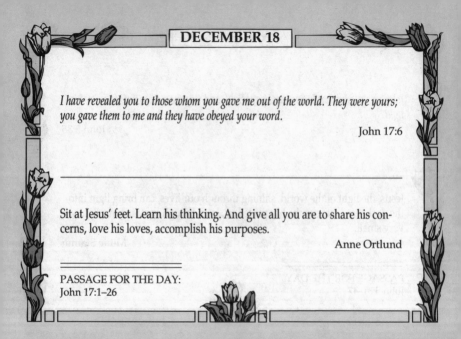

DECEMBER 18

I have revealed you to those whom you gave me out of the world. They were yours; you gave them to me and they have obeyed your word.

John 17:6

Sit at Jesus' feet. Learn his thinking. And give all you are to share his concerns, love his loves, accomplish his purposes.

Anne Ortlund

PASSAGE FOR THE DAY:
John 17:1–26

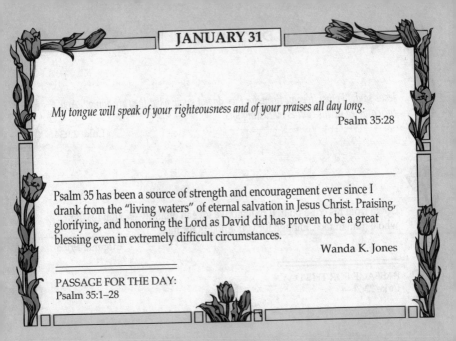

JANUARY 31

My tongue will speak of your righteousness and of your praises all day long.

Psalm 35:28

Psalm 35 has been a source of strength and encouragement ever since I drank from the "living waters" of eternal salvation in Jesus Christ. Praising, glorifying, and honoring the Lord as David did has proven to be a great blessing even in extremely difficult circumstances.

Wanda K. Jones

PASSAGE FOR THE DAY:
Psalm 35:1–28

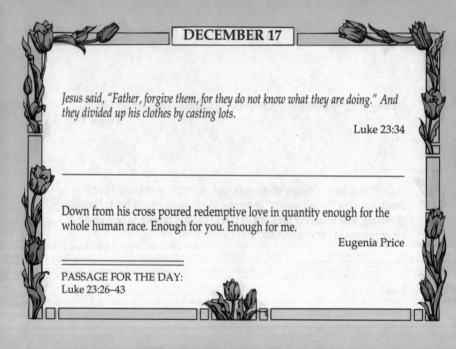

Jesus said, "Father, forgive them, for they do not know what they are doing." And they divided up his clothes by casting lots.

Luke 23:34

Down from his cross poured redemptive love in quantity enough for the whole human race. Enough for you. Enough for me.

Eugenia Price

PASSAGE FOR THE DAY:
Luke 23:26–43

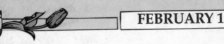

FEBRUARY 1

For God did not give us a spirit of timidity, but a spirit of power, of love and of self-discipline.

2 Timothy 1:7

I began to realize that my fears and anxieties were self-imposed. God's choice for me was to have power, love and self-discipline. God did not give me a spirit of fear! My poor self-image, my anxieties, my fears were all my own doing and my sin because I lacked faith to receive the power, love and self-discipline that God really wanted me to have.

Beverly LaHaye

PASSAGE FOR THE DAY:
2 Timothy 1:3–7

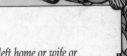

DECEMBER 16

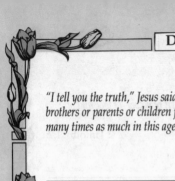

"I tell you the truth," Jesus said to them, "no one who has left home or wife or brothers or parents or children for the sake of the kingdom of God will fail to receive many times as much in this age and, in the age to come, eternal life."

Luke 18:29–30

She who had been my sister for fifty-two years had left me. A Russian woman now claimed my love. And there would be others, too, who would be my sisters and brothers in Christ all around the world.

Corrie ten Boom

PASSAGE FOR THE DAY:
Luke 18:18–30

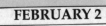

FEBRUARY 2

The elder, To the chosen lady and her children, whom I love in the truth—and not I only, but also all who know the truth. The children of your chosen sister send their greetings.

2 John 1,13

How often we wish the Bible offered more details about individuals and events, and in this letter we are left to wonder about an unnamed, unidentified woman and her "chosen sister." In one sense, it is their lack of identity that allows them to better represent the countless "chosen ladies" from around the world who have faithfully served the Lord through the centuries—women whose names have been lost in the annals of history.

Ruth A. Tucker

PASSAGE FOR THE DAY:
2 John 1–13

Then should not this woman, a daughter of Abraham, whom Satan has kept bound for eighteen long years, be set free on the Sabbath day from what bound her?

Luke 13:16

It's awfully important how you talk to people. Jesus always seemed to say the right thing the right way! He used the language of love, and so must we if we would follow in his steps and if we would see anything accomplished.

Jill Briscoe

PASSAGE FOR THE DAY:
Luke 13:10–17

FEBRUARY 3

So in the course of time Hannah conceived and gave birth to a son. She named him Samuel, saying, "Because I asked the LORD for him."

1 Samuel 1:20

There is no one holy like the LORD; there is no one besides you; there is no Rock like our God. For the foundations of the earth are the LORD's; upon them he has set the world.

Hannah

PASSAGE FOR THE DAY:
1 Samuel 1:1–20

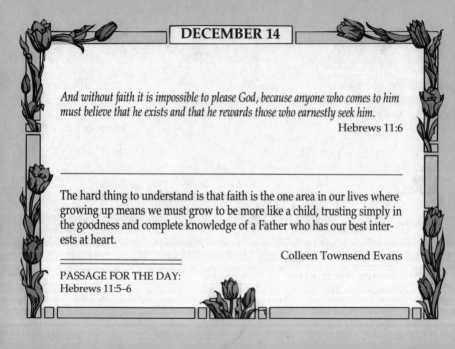

And without faith it is impossible to please God, because anyone who comes to him must believe that he exists and that he rewards those who earnestly seek him.

Hebrews 11:6

The hard thing to understand is that faith is the one area in our lives where growing up means we must grow to be more like a child, trusting simply in the goodness and complete knowledge of a Father who has our best interests at heart.

Colleen Townsend Evans

PASSAGE FOR THE DAY:
Hebrews 11:5–6

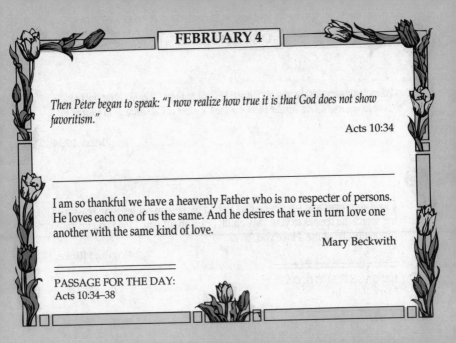

Then Peter began to speak: "I now realize how true it is that God does not show favoritism."

Acts 10:34

I am so thankful we have a heavenly Father who is no respecter of persons. He loves each one of us the same. And he desires that we in turn love one another with the same kind of love.

Mary Beckwith

PASSAGE FOR THE DAY:
Acts 10:34–38

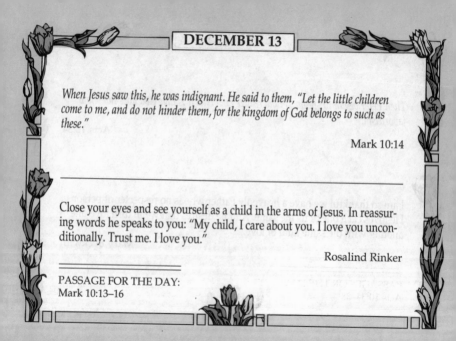

When Jesus saw this, he was indignant. He said to them, "Let the little children come to me, and do not hinder them, for the kingdom of God belongs to such as these."

Mark 10:14

Close your eyes and see yourself as a child in the arms of Jesus. In reassuring words he speaks to you: "My child, I care about you. I love you unconditionally. Trust me. I love you."

Rosalind Rinker

PASSAGE FOR THE DAY:
Mark 10:13–16

For you were once darkness, but now you are light in the Lord. Live as children of light.

Ephesians 5:8

Let's pursue that which is good, right and truthful by shining through darkened circumstances. Don't keep the switch off or hold back as though our batteries have run down. Our source is the glorious "Light Invisible." Being switched on pleased the Lord. Stay on. Stay bright.

Luci Swindoll

PASSAGE FOR THE DAY:
Ephesians 5:8–10

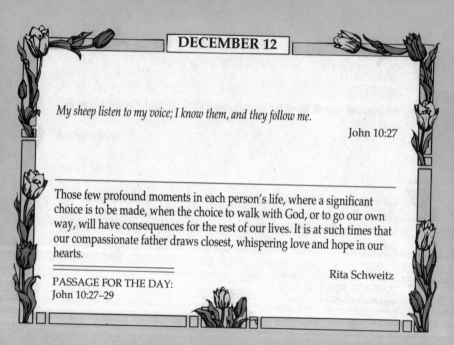

My sheep listen to my voice; I know them, and they follow me.

John 10:27

Those few profound moments in each person's life, where a significant choice is to be made, when the choice to walk with God, or to go our own way, will have consequences for the rest of our lives. It is at such times that our compassionate father draws closest, whispering love and hope in our hearts.

Rita Schweitz

PASSAGE FOR THE DAY:
John 10:27–29

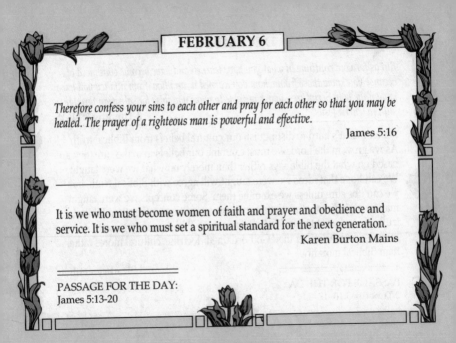

FEBRUARY 6

Therefore confess your sins to each other and pray for each other so that you may be healed. The prayer of a righteous man is powerful and effective.

James 5:16

It is we who must become women of faith and prayer and obedience and service. It is we who must set a spiritual standard for the next generation.

Karen Burton Mains

PASSAGE FOR THE DAY:
James 5:13–20

DECEMBER 11

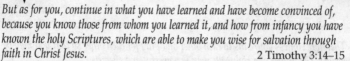

But as for you, continue in what you have learned and have become convinced of, because you know those from whom you learned it, and how from infancy you have known the holy Scriptures, which are able to make you wise for salvation through faith in Christ Jesus.   2 Timothy 3:14–15

Sometimes it's hard to distinguish our cultural beliefs from Biblical truth. As we grow in the Lord, we must examine our beliefs to make sure they are based on what the Bible says rather than merely on what we were taught. We can hope that ideas we were taught will agree with Biblical truth, but we can't be sure unless we examine them. Some concepts we were taught may be prejudices rather than convictions, traditions rather than Biblical truth. If we do not test our beliefs against the Bible, we may perpetuate human opinions rather than God-ordained doctrine, cultural mores rather than Biblical morality.

Kathryn Hillen

PASSAGE FOR THE DAY:
2 Timothy 3:10–17

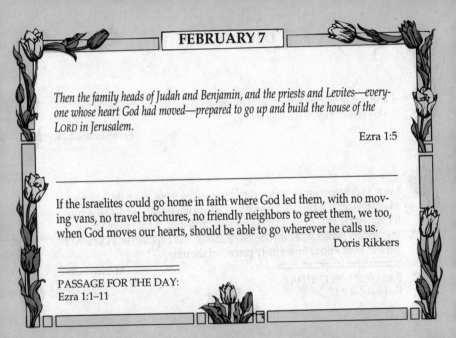

FEBRUARY 7

Then the family heads of Judah and Benjamin, and the priests and Levites—everyone whose heart God had moved—prepared to go up and build the house of the LORD in Jerusalem.

Ezra 1:5

If the Israelites could go home in faith where God led them, with no moving vans, no travel brochures, no friendly neighbors to greet them, we too, when God moves our hearts, should be able to go wherever he calls us.

Doris Rikkers

PASSAGE FOR THE DAY:
Ezra 1:1–11

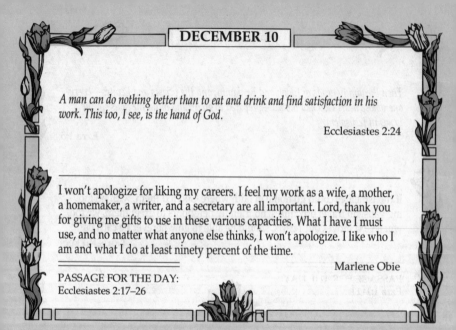

DECEMBER 10

A man can do nothing better than to eat and drink and find satisfaction in his work. This too, I see, is the hand of God.

Ecclesiastes 2:24

I won't apologize for liking my careers. I feel my work as a wife, a mother, a homemaker, a writer, and a secretary are all important. Lord, thank you for giving me gifts to use in these various capacities. What I have I must use, and no matter what anyone else thinks, I won't apologize. I like who I am and what I do at least ninety percent of the time.

Marlene Obie

PASSAGE FOR THE DAY:
Ecclesiastes 2:17–26

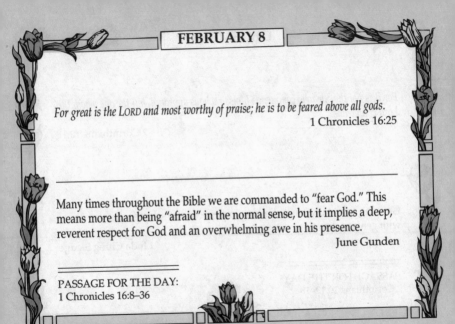

For great is the LORD and most worthy of praise; he is to be feared above all gods.
1 Chronicles 16:25

Many times throughout the Bible we are commanded to "fear God." This means more than being "afraid" in the normal sense, but it implies a deep, reverent respect for God and an overwhelming awe in his presence.

June Gunden

PASSAGE FOR THE DAY:
1 Chronicles 16:8–36

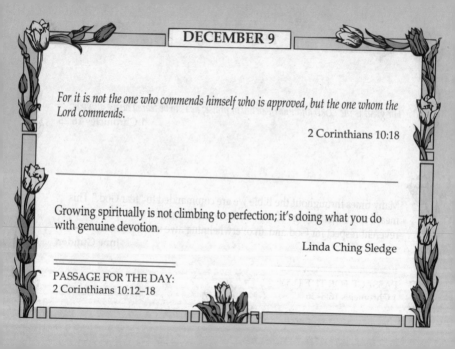

DECEMBER 9

For it is not the one who commends himself who is approved, but the one whom the Lord commends.

2 Corinthians 10:18

Growing spiritually is not climbing to perfection; it's doing what you do with genuine devotion.

Linda Ching Sledge

PASSAGE FOR THE DAY:
2 Corinthians 10:12–18

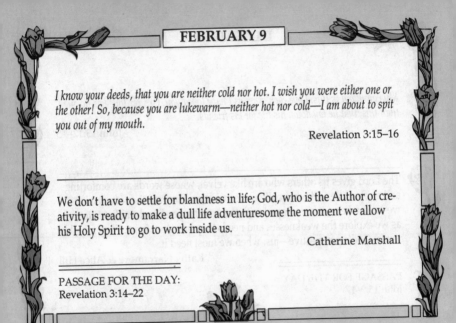

FEBRUARY 9

I know your deeds, that you are neither cold nor hot. I wish you were either one or the other! So, because you are lukewarm—neither hot nor cold—I am about to spit you out of my mouth.

Revelation 3:15–16

We don't have to settle for blandness in life; God, who is the Author of creativity, is ready to make a dull life adventuresome the moment we allow his Holy Spirit to go to work inside us.

Catherine Marshall

PASSAGE FOR THE DAY:
Revelation 3:14–22

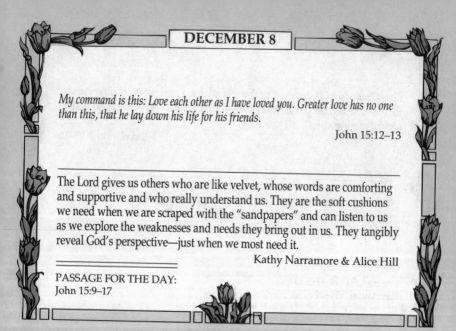

DECEMBER 8

My command is this: Love each other as I have loved you. Greater love has no one than this, that he lay down his life for his friends.

John 15:12–13

The Lord gives us others who are like velvet, whose words are comforting and supportive and who really understand us. They are the soft cushions we need when we are scraped with the "sandpapers" and can listen to us as we explore the weaknesses and needs they bring out in us. They tangibly reveal God's perspective—just when we most need it.

Kathy Narramore & Alice Hill

PASSAGE FOR THE DAY:
John 15:9–17

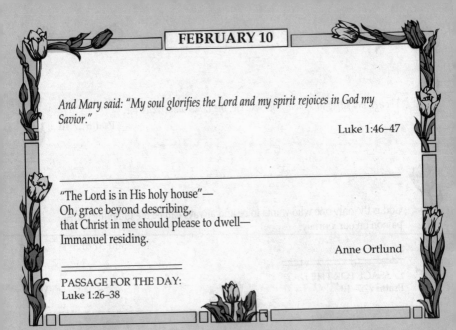

FEBRUARY 10

And Mary said: "My soul glorifies the Lord and my spirit rejoices in God my Savior."

Luke 1:46–47

"The Lord is in His holy house"—
Oh, grace beyond describing,
that Christ in me should please to dwell—
Immanuel residing.

Anne Ortlund

PASSAGE FOR THE DAY:
Luke 1:26–38

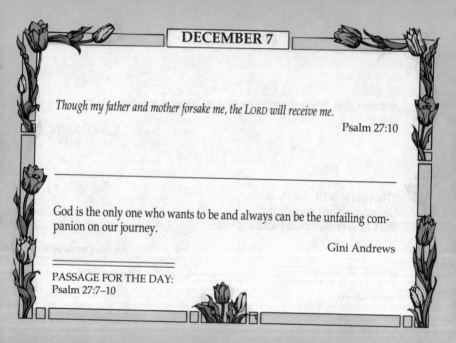

Though my father and mother forsake me, the LORD will receive me.

Psalm 27:10

God is the only one who wants to be and always can be the unfailing companion on our journey.

Gini Andrews

PASSAGE FOR THE DAY:
Psalm 27:7–10

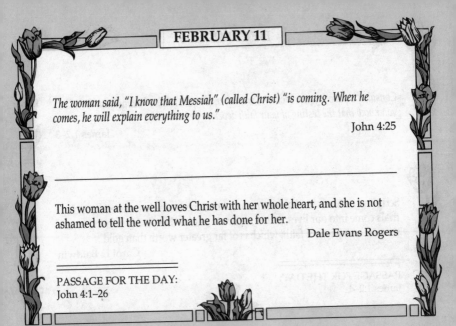

FEBRUARY 11

The woman said, "I know that Messiah" (called Christ) "is coming. When he comes, he will explain everything to us."

John 4:25

This woman at the well loves Christ with her whole heart, and she is not ashamed to tell the world what he has done for her.

Dale Evans Rogers

PASSAGE FOR THE DAY:
John 4:1–26

DECEMBER 6

Consider it pure joy, my brothers, whenever you face trials of many kinds, because you know that the testing of your faith develops perseverance.

James 1:2–3

Scripture reminds us that we are not to be surprised when suffering and trials come into our lives; rather we are to rejoice that God is refining in us the precious jewel of faith, which is of far greater worth than gold.

Carol L. Baldwin

PASSAGE FOR THE DAY:
James 1:2–4

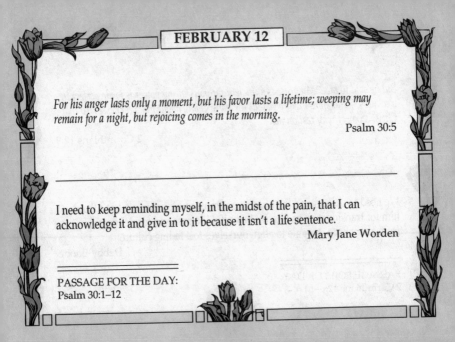

FEBRUARY 12

For his anger lasts only a moment, but his favor lasts a lifetime; weeping may remain for a night, but rejoicing comes in the morning.

Psalm 30:5

I need to keep reminding myself, in the midst of the pain, that I can acknowledge it and give in to it because it isn't a life sentence.

Mary Jane Worden

PASSAGE FOR THE DAY:
Psalm 30:1–12

DECEMBER 5

But he said to me, "My grace is sufficient for you, for my power is made perfect in weakness." Therefore I will boast all the more gladly about my weaknesses, so that Christ's power may rest on me.

2 Corinthians 12:9

We need to understand the Lord as our most worthy pursuit. Let's thank him for transforming us into his beautiful likeness and for delivering us from a stubborn struggle to align ourselves to a fading culture.

Debby Boone

PASSAGE FOR THE DAY:
2 Corinthians 12:6–10

FEBRUARY 13

*"Now, O L*ORD*, take away my life, for it is better for me to die than to live." But the L*ORD *replied, "Have you any right to be angry?"*

Jonah 4:3–4

Life isn't always the way we want it to be; it doesn't always seem fair, in our eyes or from our perspective, that is. But all is fair and just in God's eyes. And we must resist the urge to doubt or judge like Jonah.

Doris Rikkers

PASSAGE FOR THE DAY:
Jonah 4:1–11

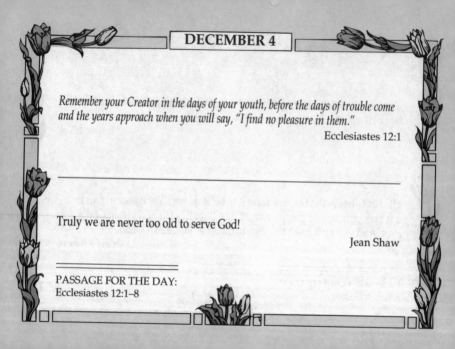

DECEMBER 4

Remember your Creator in the days of your youth, before the days of trouble come and the years approach when you will say, "I find no pleasure in them."

Ecclesiastes 12:1

Truly we are never too old to serve God!

Jean Shaw

PASSAGE FOR THE DAY:
Ecclesiastes 12:1–8

FEBRUARY 14

Heal the sick, raise the dead, cleanse those who have leprosy, drive out demons. Freely you have received, freely give.

Matthew 10:8

The next time you want to give a gift to someone you love, don't worry about how much you can afford. Consider, instead, what generosity really means: understanding. That's something each of us can afford to give—all the time.

Phyllis Hobe

PASSAGE FOR THE DAY:
Matthew 10:1–16

DECEMBER 3

A friend loves at all times, and a brother is born for adversity.

Proverbs 17:17

Friendship gives license to show up at the door of need without asking, "When would you like me to come?"... Practiced friendship whispers, "I'll be there" and promptly steps through the door with sensitivity, respect, and understanding.... Need waits with longing for the familiar entrance of dear ones who pad barefoot through the soul on ordinary days.

Susan L. Lenzkes

PASSAGE FOR THE DAY:
Proverbs 17:14–22

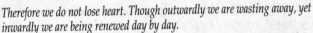

FEBRUARY 15

Therefore we do not lose heart. Though outwardly we are wasting away, yet inwardly we are being renewed day by day.

2 Corinthians 4:16

When your soul feels like a gray February day, and all seems to be rain, fog and chill drizzle, the overcast can be lifted if you will learn to just "keepin' talkin'" with God.

Karen Burton Mains

PASSAGE FOR THE DAY:
2 Corinthians 4:1-18

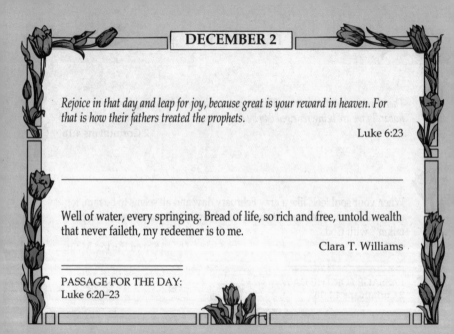

DECEMBER 2

Rejoice in that day and leap for joy, because great is your reward in heaven. For that is how their fathers treated the prophets.

Luke 6:23

Well of water, every springing. Bread of life, so rich and free, untold wealth that never faileth, my redeemer is to me.

Clara T. Williams

PASSAGE FOR THE DAY:
Luke 6:20–23

FEBRUARY 16

But a Samaritan, as he traveled, came where the man was; and when he saw him, he took pity on him.

Luke 10:33

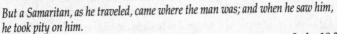

Whether it is a tiny sliver in a chubby finger, or cancer clawing at a ravaged frame, pain demands priority. Why then am I so hesitant in dispensing consolation? Must I first suffer physically, mentally, emotionally, or spiritually before I learn the healing value of a soothing hand, a mutual tear, a sympathizing heart, an understanding word?

Alma Barkman

PASSAGE FOR THE DAY:
Luke 10:25–37

DECEMBER 1

Then he sent out a dove to see if the water had receded from the surface of the ground. But the dove could find no place to set its feet because there was water over all the surface of the earth; so it returned to Noah in the ark. He reached out his hand and took the dove and brought it back to himself in the ark.

Genesis 8:8–9

There is Someone who cares about us, who watches closely for each individual: GOD! Through him we can find rest in spite of the catastrophes that harass the world. He offers us a place to stand, and hope, even in an apparently lost world. He offers a new beginning to those of us who return to him.

Gien Karssen

PASSAGE FOR THE DAY:
Genesis 8:1–12

FEBRUARY 17

Finally, be strong in the Lord and in his mighty power.

Ephesians 6:10

What does it mean to go through life with Jesus? I can answer from experience, "It works, it works!" Lord, what joy that we may tell other people that it works.

Corrie ten Boom

PASSAGE FOR THE DAY:
Ephesians 6:10–18

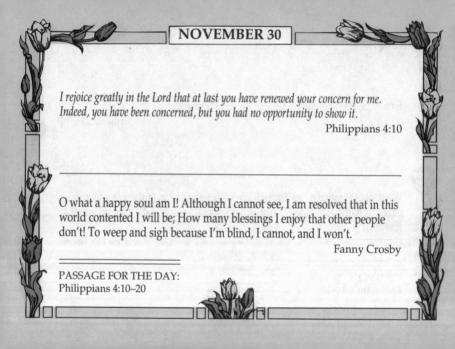

I rejoice greatly in the Lord that at last you have renewed your concern for me. Indeed, you have been concerned, but you had no opportunity to show it.

Philippians 4:10

O what a happy soul am I! Although I cannot see, I am resolved that in this world contented I will be; How many blessings I enjoy that other people don't! To weep and sigh because I'm blind, I cannot, and I won't.

Fanny Crosby

PASSAGE FOR THE DAY:
Philippians 4:10–20

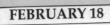

FEBRUARY 18

Then Manoah prayed to the LORD: "O Lord, I beg you, let the man of God you sent to us come again to teach us how to bring up the boy who is to be born."

Judges 13:8

Now, I can't say as I've asked lately for an angelic visit for help in raising my family, but I've certainly called on, even cried out to, God for help. And his "angels" have come to my aid in the most unexpected ways: An elderly neighbor woman who tells me what wonderful kids I've got. My mom who calls and encourages me. Maybe they don't wear wings, but they were certainly God's "angels" in answer to my call for help.

Jean E. Syswerda

PASSAGE FOR THE DAY:
Judges 13:1–14

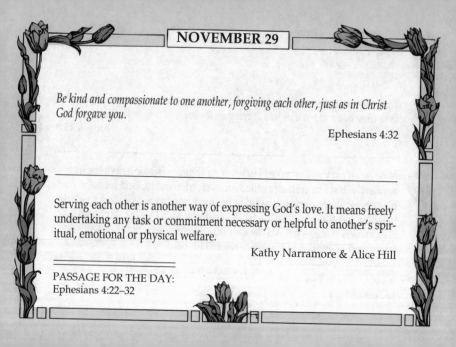

NOVEMBER 29

Be kind and compassionate to one another, forgiving each other, just as in Christ God forgave you.

Ephesians 4:32

Serving each other is another way of expressing God's love. It means freely undertaking any task or commitment necessary or helpful to another's spiritual, emotional or physical welfare.

Kathy Narramore & Alice Hill

PASSAGE FOR THE DAY:
Ephesians 4:22–32

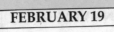

FEBRUARY 19

Praise be to the LORD your God, who has delighted in you and placed you on the throne of Israel. Because of the LORD's eternal love for Israel, he has made you king, to maintain justice and righteousness.

1 Kings 10:9

After all these centuries, the Queen of Sheba is still remembered. I'd like to take her as a role model. Honesty, giving credit, praising God—all traits that will help me daily, and, I like to think, keep me a nice memory in the minds of others.

Samantha McGarrity

PASSAGE FOR THE DAY:
1 Kings 10:1–13

But these are written that you may believe that Jesus is the Christ, the Son of God, and that by believing you may have life in his name.

John 20:31

The great artists keep us from frozenness, from smugness, from thinking that the truth is in us, rather than in God, in Christ our Lord. They help us to know that we are often closer to God in our doubts than in our certainties, that it is all right to be like the small child who constantly asks: Why? Why? Why?

Madeleine L'Engle

PASSAGE FOR THE DAY:
John 20:19–31

FEBRUARY 20

We have not received the spirit of the world but the Spirit who is from God, that we may understand what God has freely given us.

1 Corinthians 2:12

You were designed to shine; but you can never shine with your own power. The Holy Spirit provides the power to produce the light. And once you shine as you were intended to shine, you will never be useless!

June Hunt

PASSAGE FOR THE DAY:
1 Corinthians 2:11–16

Remain in me, and I will remain in you. No branch can bear fruit by itself; it must remain in the vine. Neither can you bear fruit unless you remain in me.

John 15:4

Trials are occasions for joy because they will test our faith and develop in us perseverance and maturity.

Carol L. Baldwin

PASSAGE FOR THE DAY:
John 15:1–6

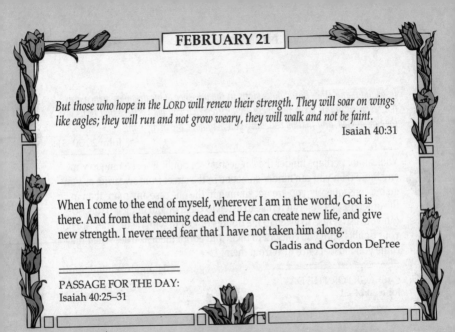

FEBRUARY 21

But those who hope in the LORD will renew their strength. They will soar on wings like eagles; they will run and not grow weary, they will walk and not be faint.

Isaiah 40:31

When I come to the end of myself, wherever I am in the world, God is there. And from that seeming dead end He can create new life, and give new strength. I never need fear that I have not taken him along.

Gladis and Gordon DePree

PASSAGE FOR THE DAY:
Isaiah 40:25–31

NOVEMBER 26

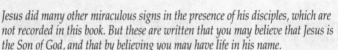

Jesus did many other miraculous signs in the presence of his disciples, which are not recorded in this book. But these are written that you may believe that Jesus is the Son of God, and that by believing you may have life in his name.

John 20:30–31

You cannot perhaps hinder the suggestions of doubt from coming to you any more than you can hinder someone in the street from swearing as you go by; consequently you are not sinning in the one case any more than in the other. Just as you can refuse to listen to them or join in their oaths, so can you also refuse to listen to the doubts or join in with them. They are not your doubts until you consent to them and adopt them as true. When they come you must at once turn from them.

Hannah Whitall Smith

PASSAGE FOR THE DAY:
John 20:24–31

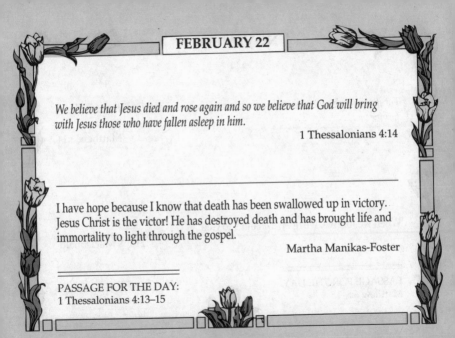

We believe that Jesus died and rose again and so we believe that God will bring with Jesus those who have fallen asleep in him.

1 Thessalonians 4:14

I have hope because I know that death has been swallowed up in victory. Jesus Christ is the victor! He has destroyed death and has brought life and immortality to light through the gospel.

Martha Manikas-Foster

PASSAGE FOR THE DAY:
1 Thessalonians 4:13–15

For if you forgive men when they sin against you, your heavenly Father will also forgive you.

Matthew 6:14

When we forgive, we open a channel to God.

Hope MacDonald

PASSAGE FOR THE DAY:
Matthew 6:5–15

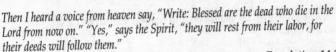

Then I heard a voice from heaven say, "Write: Blessed are the dead who die in the Lord from now on." "Yes," says the Spirit, "they will rest from their labor, for their deeds will follow them."

Revelation 14:13

Human beings are free to live their lives according to their own choices. But they have to keep in mind that there will be a future settling of accounts. All will—justly—be rewarded according to their deeds. The measuring staff will be administered according to their attitude toward the Lord Jesus Christ.

Gien Karssen

PASSAGE FOR THE DAY:
Revelation 14:6–13

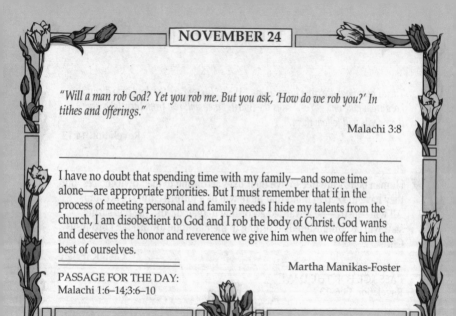

"Will a man rob God? Yet you rob me. But you ask, 'How do we rob you?' In tithes and offerings."

Malachi 3:8

I have no doubt that spending time with my family—and some time alone—are appropriate priorities. But I must remember that if in the process of meeting personal and family needs I hide my talents from the church, I am disobedient to God and I rob the body of Christ. God wants and deserves the honor and reverence we give him when we offer him the best of ourselves.

Martha Manikas-Foster

PASSAGE FOR THE DAY:
Malachi 1:6–14;3:6–10

FEBRUARY 24

Nehemiah said, "Go and enjoy choice food and sweet drinks, and send some to those who have nothing prepared. This day is sacred to our Lord. Do not grieve, for the joy of the LORD is your strength."

Nehemiah 8:10

Isn't life glorious! Isn't it grand!
Here—take it—hold it tight in your hand;
Squeeze every drop of it into your soul,
Drink of the joy of it, sun-sweet and whole!
Laugh with the love of it, burst into song!
Scatter its richness as you stride along!
Isn't life splendid—and isn't it great
We can always start living—it's never too late!

Helen Lowrie Marshall

PASSAGE FOR THE DAY:
Nehemiah 8:7–10

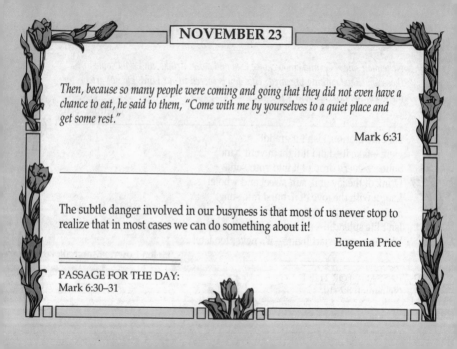

Then, because so many people were coming and going that they did not even have a chance to eat, he said to them, "Come with me by yourselves to a quiet place and get some rest."

Mark 6:31

The subtle danger involved in our busyness is that most of us never stop to realize that in most cases we can do something about it!

Eugenia Price

PASSAGE FOR THE DAY:
Mark 6:30–31

FEBRUARY 25

"Do not come any closer," God said. "Take off your sandals, for the place where you are standing is holy ground."

Exodus 3:5

Oh, praise the Lord!
"This earth is crammed with heaven!"
Oh, praise the Lord!
And, Christian, look around!
For every bush you pass with fire is flaming,
And every spot you tread is holy ground.

Anne Ortlund

PASSAGE FOR THE DAY:
Exodus 3:1–5

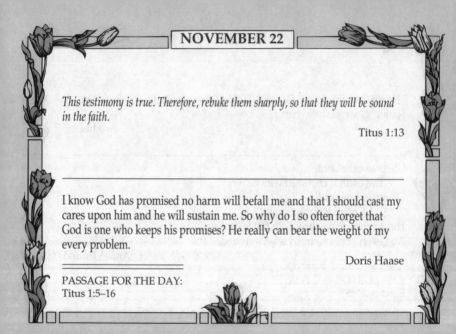

NOVEMBER 22

This testimony is true. Therefore, rebuke them sharply, so that they will be sound in the faith.

Titus 1:13

I know God has promised no harm will befall me and that I should cast my cares upon him and he will sustain me. So why do I so often forget that God is one who keeps his promises? He really can bear the weight of my every problem.

Doris Haase

PASSAGE FOR THE DAY:
Titus 1:5–16

FEBRUARY 26

You see, at just the right time, when we were still powerless, Christ died for the ungodly.

Romans 5:6

No scholar, yet a teacher. For though I can't recall the character he described, it captured my mind. It makes me think of you, my Lord hanging between heaven and hell, heartstrings stretched so tight they snapped, so forsaken that you cried "Oh, my God!" to empty, silent skies. All alone by yourself and nobody with you. For me.

Joan Rae Mills

PASSAGE FOR THE DAY:
Romans 5:6–8

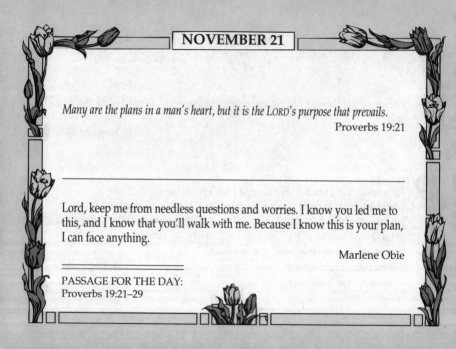

Many are the plans in a man's heart, but it is the LORD's purpose that prevails.

Proverbs 19:21

Lord, keep me from needless questions and worries. I know you led me to this, and I know that you'll walk with me. Because I know this is your plan, I can face anything.

Marlene Obie

PASSAGE FOR THE DAY:
Proverbs 19:21–29

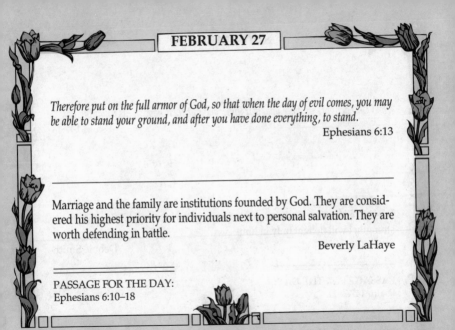

FEBRUARY 27

Therefore put on the full armor of God, so that when the day of evil comes, you may be able to stand your ground, and after you have done everything, to stand.

Ephesians 6:13

Marriage and the family are institutions founded by God. They are considered his highest priority for individuals next to personal salvation. They are worth defending in battle.

Beverly LaHaye

PASSAGE FOR THE DAY:
Ephesians 6:10–18

NOVEMBER 20

The LORD delights in those who fear him, who put their hope in his unfailing love.

Psalm 147:11

I desire only to fear God and put my hope in his love . . . and through his strength, I will delight only in him!

Debbie Smith

PASSAGE FOR THE DAY:
Psalm 147:7–11

FEBRUARY 28

We proclaim to you what we have seen and heard, so that you also may have fellowship with us. And our fellowship is with the Father and with his Son, Jesus Christ. We write this to make our joy complete.

1 John 1:3–4

Talking with others about Jesus is always risky. You may risk turning them off. But it is worth the risk, because it will bring that complete joy you desperately desire.

Rosemary Jensen

PASSAGE FOR THE DAY:
1 John 1:1–10

NOVEMBER 19

You then, my son, be strong in the grace that is in Christ Jesus.

2 Timothy 2:1

How much lighter trials become when we realize God's grace is twofold. It is not only the happy ending. It is also the peace we can feel during a painful journey, when we trust in God—all the way.

Doris Haase

PASSAGE FOR THE DAY:
2 Timothy 2:1–13

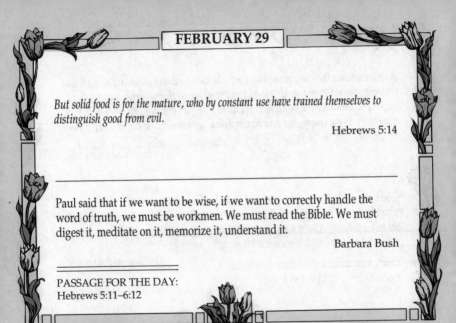

FEBRUARY 29

But solid food is for the mature, who by constant use have trained themselves to distinguish good from evil.

Hebrews 5:14

Paul said that if we want to be wise, if we want to correctly handle the word of truth, we must be workmen. We must read the Bible. We must digest it, meditate on it, memorize it, understand it.

Barbara Bush

PASSAGE FOR THE DAY:
Hebrews 5:11–6:12

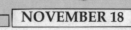

NOVEMBER 18

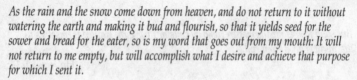

As the rain and the snow come down from heaven, and do not return to it without watering the earth and making it bud and flourish, so that it yields seed for the sower and bread for the eater, so is my word that goes out from my mouth: It will not return to me empty, but will accomplish what I desire and achieve that purpose for which I sent it.

Isaiah 55:10–11

God never takes away except to give us back something better. It means we must be brave enough and determined enough to wait . . . because it often takes God time to turn a painful situation to good. We can embrace our pain and not resent it because a blessing is coming!

Ann Kiemel Anderson

PASSAGE FOR THE DAY:
Isaiah 55:8–11

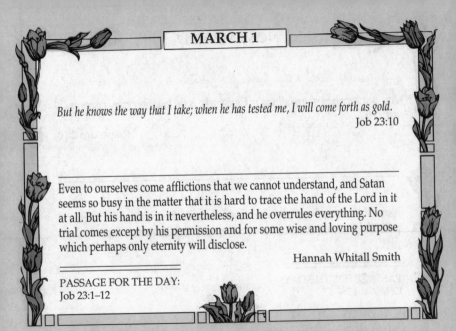

MARCH 1

But he knows the way that I take; when he has tested me, I will come forth as gold.

Job 23:10

Even to ourselves come afflictions that we cannot understand, and Satan seems so busy in the matter that it is hard to trace the hand of the Lord in it at all. But his hand is in it nevertheless, and he overrules everything. No trial comes except by his permission and for some wise and loving purpose which perhaps only eternity will disclose.

Hannah Whitall Smith

PASSAGE FOR THE DAY:
Job 23:1–12

And you have been given fullness in Christ, who is the head over every power and authority.

Colossians 2:10

Jesus Christ is the head over every power and authority, and he is more powerful than sorrow, gloom, fear, insecurity and the need for approval.

Marie Chapian

PASSAGE FOR THE DAY:
Colossians 2:6–12

MARCH 2

Let the peace of Christ rule in your hearts, since as members of one body you were called to peace. And be thankful. Let the word of Christ dwell in you richly as you teach and admonish one another with all wisdom, and as you sing psalms, hymns and spiritual songs with gratitude in your hearts to God. And whatever you do, whether in word or deed, do it all in the name of the Lord Jesus, giving thanks to God the Father through him.

Colossians 3:15–17

When I have felt confined or frustrated, I have reached again to touch a part of God's creation. God's character is revealed, in part, through his excellent work in the details.

Martha Manikas-Foster

PASSAGE FOR THE DAY:
Colossians 3:1–17

You are all sons of God through faith in Christ Jesus.

Galatians 3:26

When I'm reminded of God's unconditional, steadfast love, it helps me fight against the prejudice that tries to creep in, distort my conception of others, and tempts me to look at myself more highly than I should.

Mary Beckwith

PASSAGE FOR THE DAY:
Galatians 3:26–28

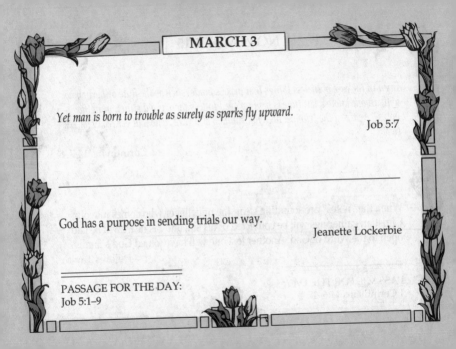

MARCH 3

Yet man is born to trouble as surely as sparks fly upward.

Job 5:7

God has a purpose in sending trials our way.

Jeanette Lockerbie

PASSAGE FOR THE DAY:
Job 5:1–9

NOVEMBER 15

Even in the case of lifeless things that make sounds, such as the flute or harp, how will anyone know what tune is being played unless there is a distinction in the notes? Again, if the trumpet does not sound a clear call, who will get ready for battle?

1 Corinthians 14:7–8

When the "notes" are sounding clear, the unbeliever who comes into our Christian gatherings will be convicted of his sin, and his heart will be laid open to the Word of God. Another lost one will have joined God's family.

Delores Taylor

PASSAGE FOR THE DAY:
1 Corinthians 14:6–12

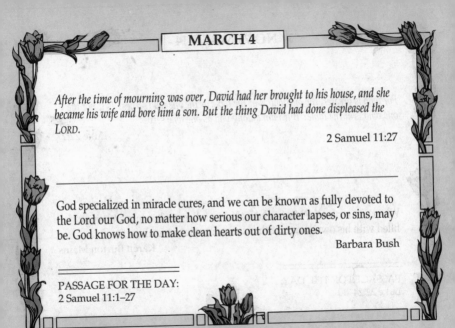

MARCH 4

After the time of mourning was over, David had her brought to his house, and she became his wife and bore him a son. But the thing David had done displeased the LORD.

2 Samuel 11:27

God specialized in miracle cures, and we can be known as fully devoted to the Lord our God, no matter how serious our character lapses, or sins, may be. God knows how to make clean hearts out of dirty ones.

Barbara Bush

PASSAGE FOR THE DAY:
2 Samuel 11:1–27

For who is greater, the one who is at the table or the one who serves? Is it not the one who is at the table? But I am among you as one who serves.

Luke 22:27

When one serves the Master, he makes us full, complete human beings filled with his own image, with his own amazing mentality.

Karen Burton Mains

PASSAGE FOR THE DAY:
Luke 22:24–30

The LORD said to him, "Who gave man his mouth? Who makes him deaf or mute? Who gives him sight or makes him blind? Is it not I, the LORD?"

Exodus 4:11

God controls all things, whether genetic mistakes or chromosome miscounts. Somehow, all these "accidents"—whether prenatal problems or injuries at birth—come under the sovereign control of God.

Joni Eareckson Tada

PASSAGE FOR THE DAY:
Exodus 4:1–31

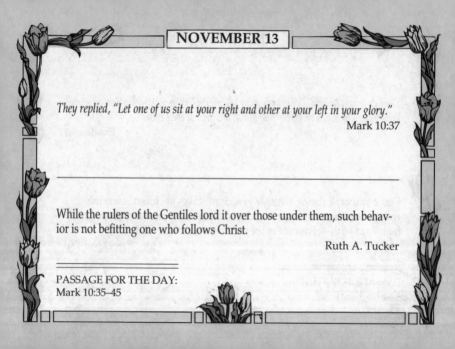

They replied, "Let one of us sit at your right and other at your left in your glory."
Mark 10:37

While the rulers of the Gentiles lord it over those under them, such behavior is not befitting one who follows Christ.

Ruth A. Tucker

PASSAGE FOR THE DAY:
Mark 10:35–45

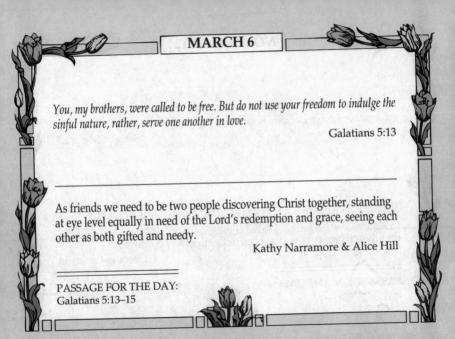

MARCH 6

You, my brothers, were called to be free. But do not use your freedom to indulge the sinful nature, rather, serve one another in love.

Galatians 5:13

As friends we need to be two people discovering Christ together, standing at eye level equally in need of the Lord's redemption and grace, seeing each other as both gifted and needy.

Kathy Narramore & Alice Hill

PASSAGE FOR THE DAY:
Galatians 5:13–15

Daughters of Jerusalem, I charge you by the gazelles and by the does of the field: Do not arouse or awaken love until it so desires.

Song of Songs 2:7

The mutual love between Solomon and the Shulammite is a beautiful example of marital bliss in physical intimacy. Nowhere else in Scripture is the physical beauty of womanhood more effectively portrayed.

Dorothy Patterson

PASSAGE FOR THE DAY:
Song of Songs 2:2–7

Do not be anxious about anything, but in everything, by prayer and petition, with thanksgiving, present your requests to God.

Philippians 4:6

I was reminded of the profound truth that prayer isn't something I had to do, rather, prayer is something I get to do. I get to bring to God every worry and concern that is on my heart today.

Hope MacDonald

PASSAGE FOR THE DAY:
Philippians 4:4–9

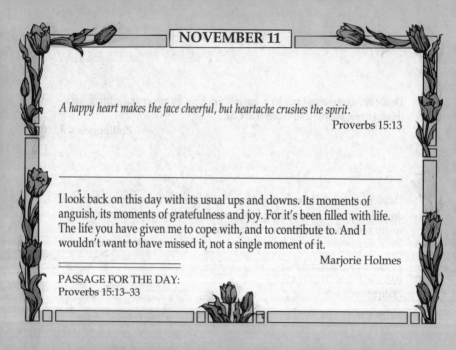

NOVEMBER 11

A happy heart makes the face cheerful, but heartache crushes the spirit.

Proverbs 15:13

I look back on this day with its usual ups and downs. Its moments of anguish, its moments of gratefulness and joy. For it's been filled with life. The life you have given me to cope with, and to contribute to. And I wouldn't want to have missed it, not a single moment of it.

Marjorie Holmes

PASSAGE FOR THE DAY:
Proverbs 15:13–33

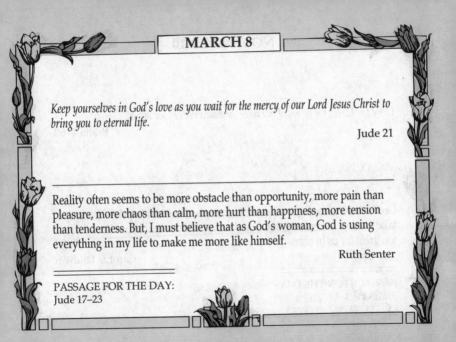

MARCH 8

Keep yourselves in God's love as you wait for the mercy of our Lord Jesus Christ to bring you to eternal life.

Jude 21

Reality often seems to be more obstacle than opportunity, more pain than pleasure, more chaos than calm, more hurt than happiness, more tension than tenderness. But, I must believe that as God's woman, God is using everything in my life to make me more like himself.

Ruth Senter

PASSAGE FOR THE DAY:
Jude 17–23

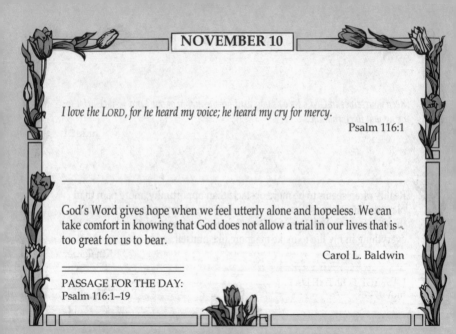

NOVEMBER 10

I love the LORD, for he heard my voice; he heard my cry for mercy.

Psalm 116:1

God's Word gives hope when we feel utterly alone and hopeless. We can take comfort in knowing that God does not allow a trial in our lives that is too great for us to bear.

Carol L. Baldwin

PASSAGE FOR THE DAY:
Psalm 116:1–19

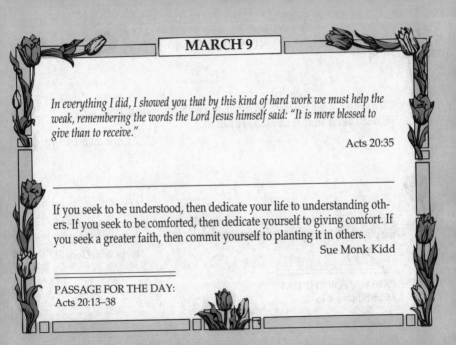

MARCH 9

In everything I did, I showed you that by this kind of hard work we must help the weak, remembering the words the Lord Jesus himself said: "It is more blessed to give than to receive."

Acts 20:35

If you seek to be understood, then dedicate your life to understanding others. If you seek to be comforted, then dedicate yourself to giving comfort. If you seek a greater faith, then commit yourself to planting it in others.

Sue Monk Kidd

PASSAGE FOR THE DAY:
Acts 20:13–38

NOVEMBER 9

Therefore we do not lose heart. Though outwardly we are wasting away, yet inwardly we are being renewed day by day.

2 Corinthians 4:16

Thank you Jesus, for your power in every part of my life today—renewing me physically, mentally and spiritually.

Hope MacDonald

PASSAGE FOR THE DAY:
2 Corinthians 4:16–18

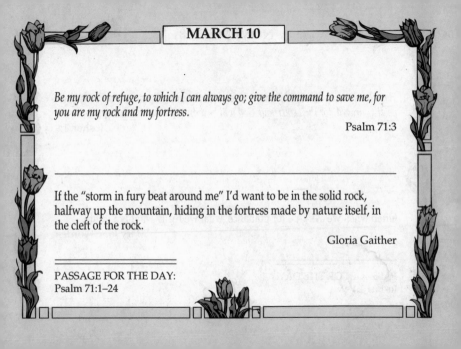

MARCH 10

Be my rock of refuge, to which I can always go; give the command to save me, for you are my rock and my fortress.

Psalm 71:3

If the "storm in fury beat around me" I'd want to be in the solid rock, halfway up the mountain, hiding in the fortress made by nature itself, in the cleft of the rock.

Gloria Gaither

PASSAGE FOR THE DAY:
Psalm 71:1–24

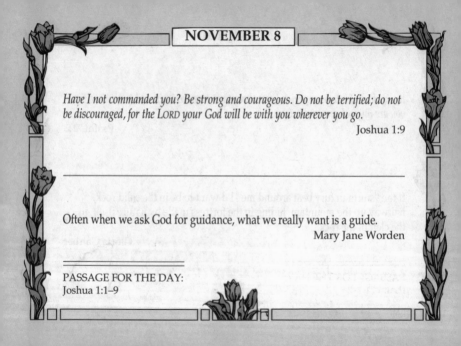

NOVEMBER 8

Have I not commanded you? Be strong and courageous. Do not be terrified; do not be discouraged, for the LORD your God will be with you wherever you go.

Joshua 1:9

Often when we ask God for guidance, what we really want is a guide.

Mary Jane Worden

PASSAGE FOR THE DAY:
Joshua 1:1–9

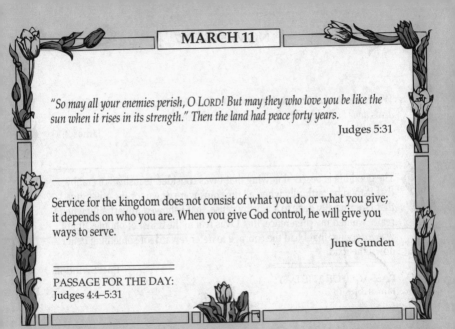

"So may all your enemies perish, O LORD! But may they who love you be like the sun when it rises in its strength." Then the land had peace forty years.

Judges 5:31

Service for the kingdom does not consist of what you do or what you give; it depends on who you are. When you give God control, he will give you ways to serve.

June Gunden

PASSAGE FOR THE DAY:
Judges 4:4–5:31

NOVEMBER 7

Who is wise and understanding among you? Let him show it by his good life, by deeds done in the humility that comes from wisdom.

James 3:13

The good life is peace—knowing that I was considerate instead of crabby, that I stood by faithfully when all the chips were down for the other guy, that I sacrificially gave to a worthy cause, that I showed impartiality when I really wanted my preference, that I was real in the midst of phonies, that I was forgiving, that I had the courage to defer reward for something better down the road.

Luci Swindoll

PASSAGE FOR THE DAY:
James 3:13–18

MARCH 12

But when she could hide him no longer, she got a papyrus basket for him and coated it with tar and pitch. Then she placed the child in it and put it among the reeds along the bank of the Nile.

Exodus 2:3

The Lord has a plan for your son or daughter. He will take notes of our efforts to deliver our own children. "Nursing them" with the Word of God; "bathing them" in prayer, who knows? We may be entrusted with a "Moses"!

Jeanette Lockerbie

PASSAGE FOR THE DAY:
Exodus 2:1–10

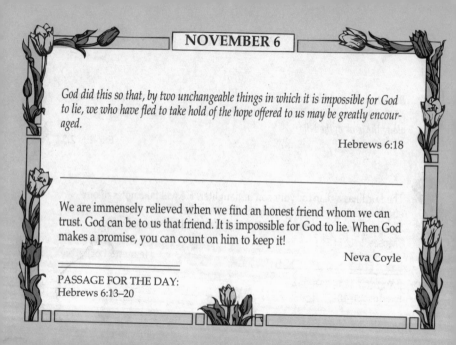

God did this so that, by two unchangeable things in which it is impossible for God to lie, we who have fled to take hold of the hope offered to us may be greatly encouraged.

Hebrews 6:18

We are immensely relieved when we find an honest friend whom we can trust. God can be to us that friend. It is impossible for God to lie. When God makes a promise, you can count on him to keep it!

Neva Coyle

PASSAGE FOR THE DAY:
Hebrews 6:13–20

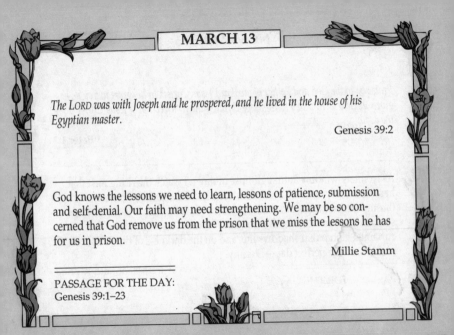

MARCH 13

The LORD was with Joseph and he prospered, and he lived in the house of his Egyptian master.

Genesis 39:2

God knows the lessons we need to learn, lessons of patience, submission and self-denial. Our faith may need strengthening. We may be so concerned that God remove us from the prison that we miss the lessons he has for us in prison.

Millie Stamm

PASSAGE FOR THE DAY:
Genesis 39:1–23

NOVEMBER 5

Praise be to the God and Father of our Lord Jesus Christ! In his great mercy he has given us new birth into a living hope through the resurrection of Jesus Christ from the dead.

1 Peter 1:3

As from my window at first glimpse of dawn I watch the rising mist that heralds the day, and see by God's strong hand the curtain drawn that through the night has hid the world away. So I, through windows of my soul shall see one day death's fingers with resistless might draw back the curtained gloom that shadows life, and on the darkness of time's deepest night, let in the perfect day—Eternity.

Alice Macdonald Kipling

PASSAGE FOR THE DAY:
1 Peter 1:3–12

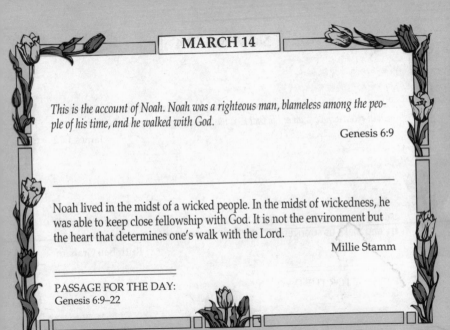

This is the account of Noah. Noah was a righteous man, blameless among the people of his time, and he walked with God.

Genesis 6:9

Noah lived in the midst of a wicked people. In the midst of wickedness, he was able to keep close fellowship with God. It is not the environment but the heart that determines one's walk with the Lord.

Millie Stamm

PASSAGE FOR THE DAY:
Genesis 6:9–22

NOVEMBER 4

Blessed is the man who perseveres under trial, because when he has stood the test, he will receive the crown of life that God has promised to those who love him.

James 1:12

Satan uses an occasion or a person to tempt us to fall; God uses the same to try and make us stronger.

Ruth Bell Graham

PASSAGE FOR THE DAY:
James 1:12–15

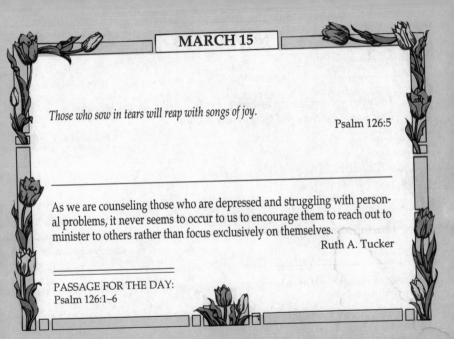

MARCH 15

Those who sow in tears will reap with songs of joy.

Psalm 126:5

As we are counseling those who are depressed and struggling with personal problems, it never seems to occur to us to encourage them to reach out to minister to others rather than focus exclusively on themselves.

Ruth A. Tucker

PASSAGE FOR THE DAY:
Psalm 126:1–6

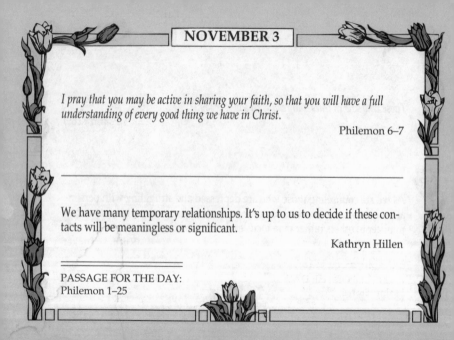

NOVEMBER 3

I pray that you may be active in sharing your faith, so that you will have a full understanding of every good thing we have in Christ.

Philemon 6–7

We have many temporary relationships. It's up to us to decide if these contacts will be meaningless or significant.

Kathryn Hillen

PASSAGE FOR THE DAY:
Philemon 1–25

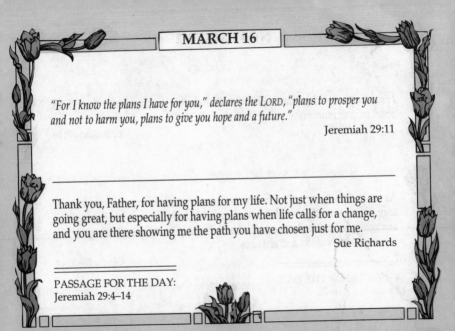

MARCH 16

"For I know the plans I have for you," declares the LORD, "plans to prosper you and not to harm you, plans to give you hope and a future."

Jeremiah 29:11

Thank you, Father, for having plans for my life. Not just when things are going great, but especially for having plans when life calls for a change, and you are there showing me the path you have chosen just for me.

Sue Richards

PASSAGE FOR THE DAY:
Jeremiah 29:4–14

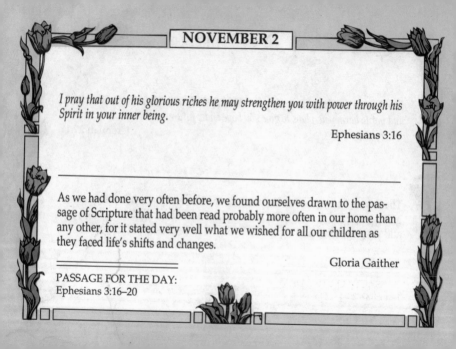

NOVEMBER 2

I pray that out of his glorious riches he may strengthen you with power through his Spirit in your inner being.

Ephesians 3:16

As we had done very often before, we found ourselves drawn to the passage of Scripture that had been read probably more often in our home than any other, for it stated very well what we wished for all our children as they faced life's shifts and changes.

Gloria Gaither

PASSAGE FOR THE DAY:
Ephesians 3:16–20

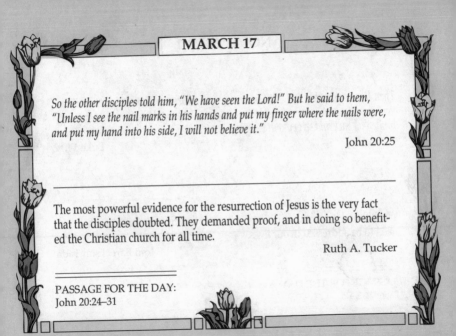

MARCH 17

So the other disciples told him, "We have seen the Lord!" But he said to them, "Unless I see the nail marks in his hands and put my finger where the nails were, and put my hand into his side, I will not believe it."

John 20:25

The most powerful evidence for the resurrection of Jesus is the very fact that the disciples doubted. They demanded proof, and in doing so benefited the Christian church for all time.

Ruth A. Tucker

PASSAGE FOR THE DAY:
John 20:24–31

NOVEMBER 1

Then Jesus said to his host, "When you give a luncheon or dinner, do not invite your friends, your brothers or relatives, or your rich neighbors; if you do, they may invite you back and so you will be repaid."

Luke 14:12

We will find it difficult to divert God's attention from those issues that need to be addressed in our lives.

Joni Eareckson Tada

PASSAGE FOR THE DAY:
Luke 14:1–35

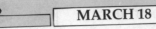

MARCH 18

Then Jesus said to his disciples, "If anyone would come after me, he must deny himself and take up his cross and follow me. For whoever wants to save his life will lose it, but whoever loses his life for me will find it."

Matthew 16:24–25

When any of us embarks on the pursuit of happiness for ourselves, it eludes us. It must be because happiness comes to us only as a dividend. When we become absorbed in something demanding and worthwhile above and beyond ourselves, happiness seems to be there as a by-product of the self-giving.

Catherine Marshall

PASSAGE FOR THE DAY:
Matthew 16:21–28

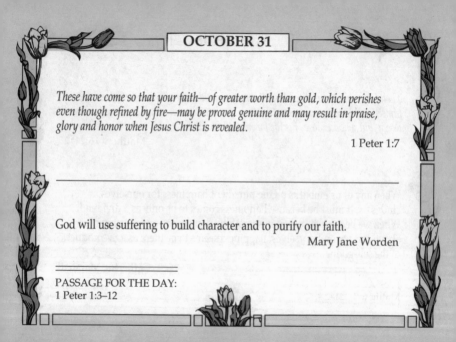

OCTOBER 31

These have come so that your faith—of greater worth than gold, which perishes even though refined by fire—may be proved genuine and may result in praise, glory and honor when Jesus Christ is revealed.

1 Peter 1:7

God will use suffering to build character and to purify our faith.

Mary Jane Worden

PASSAGE FOR THE DAY:
1 Peter 1:3–12

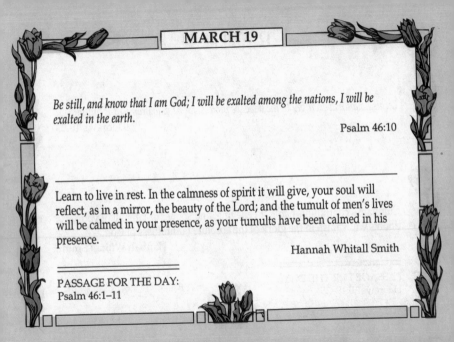

MARCH 19

Be still, and know that I am God; I will be exalted among the nations, I will be exalted in the earth.

Psalm 46:10

Learn to live in rest. In the calmness of spirit it will give, your soul will reflect, as in a mirror, the beauty of the Lord; and the tumult of men's lives will be calmed in your presence, as your tumults have been calmed in his presence.

Hannah Whitall Smith

PASSAGE FOR THE DAY:
Psalm 46:1–11

Let us hold unswervingly to the hope we profess, for he who promised is faithful.

Hebrews 10:23

Cultivate a continuous habit of believing, and sooner or later all of your doubts will vanish in the glory of the absolute faithfulness of God.

Hannah Whitall Smith

PASSAGE FOR THE DAY:
Hebrews 10:19–25

Do not gloat over me, my enemy! Though I have fallen, I will rise. Though I sit in darkness, the LORD will be my light.

Micah 7:8

Just as one small candle can dispel the darkness in an arena, so can the entrance of light into our souls dispel the bleak and dreary darkness lurking there. And how much greater that light—the light of the Lord—than one little candle.

Diane Noble

PASSAGE FOR THE DAY:
Micah 7:1–9

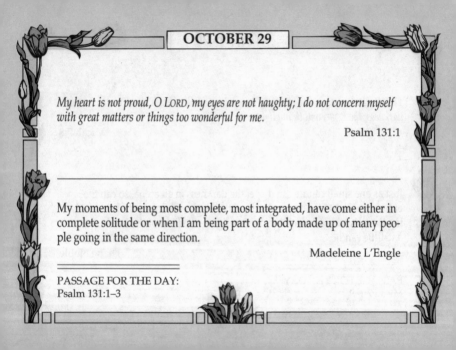

OCTOBER 29

My heart is not proud, O LORD, my eyes are not haughty; I do not concern myself with great matters or things too wonderful for me.

Psalm 131:1

My moments of being most complete, most integrated, have come either in complete solitude or when I am being part of a body made up of many people going in the same direction.

Madeleine L'Engle

PASSAGE FOR THE DAY:
Psalm 131:1–3

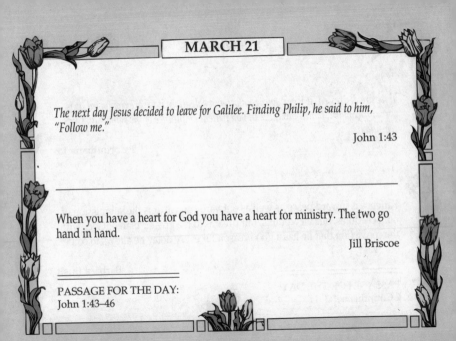

MARCH 21

The next day Jesus decided to leave for Galilee. Finding Philip, he said to him, "Follow me."

John 1:43

When you have a heart for God you have a heart for ministry. The two go hand in hand.

Jill Briscoe

PASSAGE FOR THE DAY:
John 1:43–46

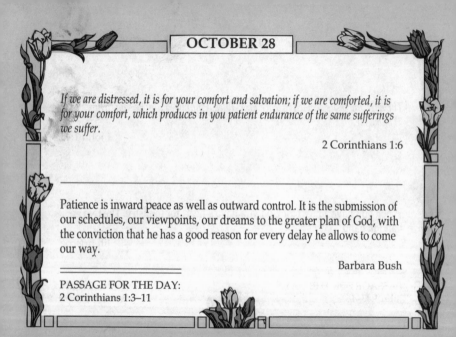

OCTOBER 28

If we are distressed, it is for your comfort and salvation; if we are comforted, it is for your comfort, which produces in you patient endurance of the same sufferings we suffer.

2 Corinthians 1:6

Patience is inward peace as well as outward control. It is the submission of our schedules, our viewpoints, our dreams to the greater plan of God, with the conviction that he has a good reason for every delay he allows to come our way.

Barbara Bush

PASSAGE FOR THE DAY:
2 Corinthians 1:3–11

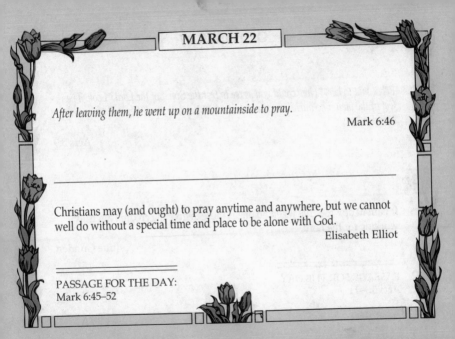

MARCH 22

After leaving them, he went up on a mountainside to pray.

Mark 6:46

Christians may (and ought) to pray anytime and anywhere, but we cannot well do without a special time and place to be alone with God.

Elisabeth Elliot

PASSAGE FOR THE DAY:
Mark 6:45–52

Peter said to her, "How could you agree to test the Spirit of the Lord? Look! The feet of the men who buried your husband are at the door, and they will carry you out also."

Acts 5:9

If I am happy to serve when no one is there to give me credit, I am truly working for the Lord.

June Gunden

PASSAGE FOR THE DAY:
Acts 5:1–11

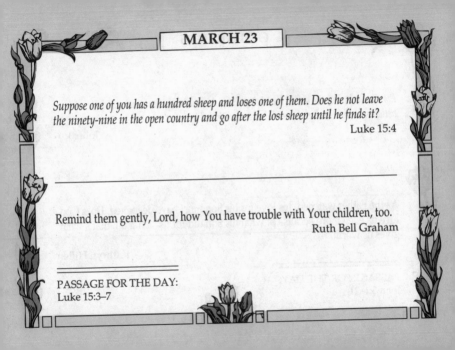

MARCH 23

Suppose one of you has a hundred sheep and loses one of them. Does he not leave the ninety-nine in the open country and go after the lost sheep until he finds it?

Luke 15:4

Remind them gently, Lord, how You have trouble with Your children, too.

Ruth Bell Graham

PASSAGE FOR THE DAY:
Luke 15:3–7

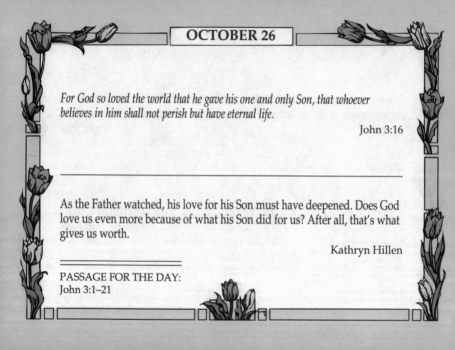

OCTOBER 26

For God so loved the world that he gave his one and only Son, that whoever believes in him shall not perish but have eternal life.

John 3:16

As the Father watched, his love for his Son must have deepened. Does God love us even more because of what his Son did for us? After all, that's what gives us worth.

Kathryn Hillen

PASSAGE FOR THE DAY:
John 3:1–21

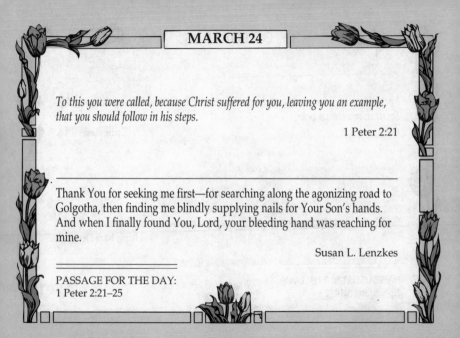

MARCH 24

To this you were called, because Christ suffered for you, leaving you an example, that you should follow in his steps.

1 Peter 2:21

Thank You for seeking me first—for searching along the agonizing road to Golgotha, then finding me blindly supplying nails for Your Son's hands. And when I finally found You, Lord, your bleeding hand was reaching for mine.

Susan L. Lenzkes

PASSAGE FOR THE DAY:
1 Peter 2:21–25

I pray that out of his glorious riches he may strengthen you with power through his Spirit in your inner being.

Ephesians 3:16

_____

God holds us responsible for our lives and what we do with them.

Hope MacDonald

PASSAGE FOR THE DAY:
Ephesians 3:14–21

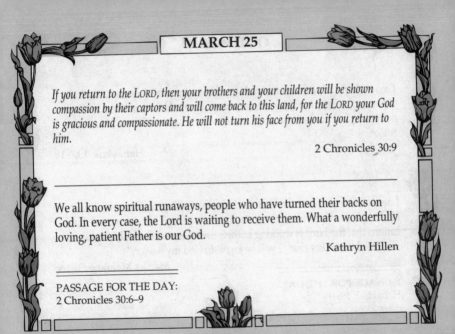

If you return to the LORD, then your brothers and your children will be shown compassion by their captors and will come back to this land, for the LORD your God is gracious and compassionate. He will not turn his face from you if you return to him.

2 Chronicles 30:9

We all know spiritual runaways, people who have turned their backs on God. In every case, the Lord is waiting to receive them. What a wonderfully loving, patient Father is our God.

Kathryn Hillen

PASSAGE FOR THE DAY:
2 Chronicles 30:6–9

OCTOBER 24

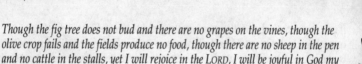

Though the fig tree does not bud and there are no grapes on the vines, though the olive crop fails and the fields produce no food, though there are no sheep in the pen and no cattle in the stalls, yet I will rejoice in the LORD, I will be joyful in God my Savior.

Habakkuk 3:17–18

I needed to learn to rest in God's sufficiency. I will probably never know God's specific plans for my friends. But even though I see no outward indications that the Lord is working in their lives, I know that he has not neglected them. For that "I will be joyful in God my Savior."

Martha Manikas-Foster

PASSAGE FOR THE DAY:
Habakkuk 3:1–19

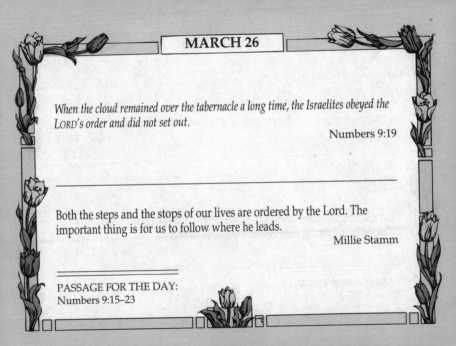

MARCH 26

When the cloud remained over the tabernacle a long time, the Israelites obeyed the LORD's *order and did not set out.*

Numbers 9:19

Both the steps and the stops of our lives are ordered by the Lord. The important thing is for us to follow where he leads.

Millie Stamm

PASSAGE FOR THE DAY:
Numbers 9:15–23

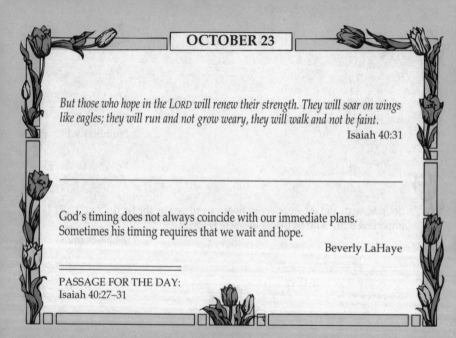

OCTOBER 23

But those who hope in the LORD will renew their strength. They will soar on wings like eagles; they will run and not grow weary, they will walk and not be faint.

Isaiah 40:31

God's timing does not always coincide with our immediate plans. Sometimes his timing requires that we wait and hope.

Beverly LaHaye

PASSAGE FOR THE DAY:
Isaiah 40:27–31

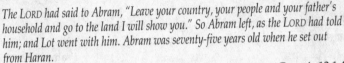

MARCH 27

The LORD had said to Abram, "Leave your country, your people and your father's household and go to the land I will show you." So Abram left, as the LORD had told him; and Lot went with him. Abram was seventy-five years old when he set out from Haran.

Genesis 12:1,4

God willingly enters into our daily lives. For this is the God of the incarnation, the God of life who joins us on earth. God willingly speaks in time and space, for this is the God who is creator: and all things, time, space, people, are the creatures of his hand.

Patricia Beall Gavigan

PASSAGE FOR THE DAY:
Genesis 12:1–9

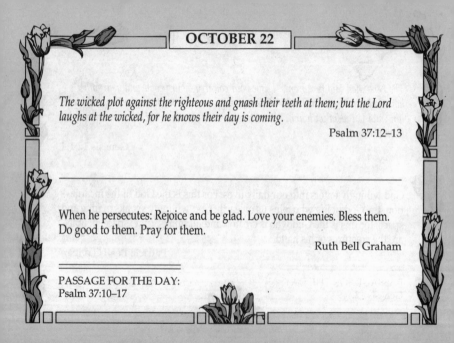

The wicked plot against the righteous and gnash their teeth at them; but the Lord laughs at the wicked, for he knows their day is coming.

Psalm 37:12–13

When he persecutes: Rejoice and be glad. Love your enemies. Bless them. Do good to them. Pray for them.

Ruth Bell Graham

PASSAGE FOR THE DAY:
Psalm 37:10–17

He said to her, "Daughter, your faith has healed you. Go in peace and be freed from your suffering."

Mark 5:34

Remember the woman of Mark 5. She sought Jesus and was determined to find him. When he did, he met her needs. He will meet yours. Ask him.

Wanda K. Jones

PASSAGE FOR THE DAY:
Mark 5:25–34

OCTOBER 21

Avoid godless chatter, because those who indulge in it will become more and more ungodly. Their teaching will spread like gangrene. Among them are Hymenaeus and Philetus.

2 Timothy 3:16–17

We need to examine our own beliefs and be responsible for what we teach others, including our children and people in our church. Growing up in Christ means listening to his voice. We must pray that the Holy Spirit will guide us and lead us into all truth.

Kathryn Hillen

PASSAGE FOR THE DAY:
2 Timothy 3:10–17

But Daniel resolved not to defile himself with the royal food and wine, and he asked the chief official for permission not to defile himself this way.

Daniel 1:8

I don't know the potential of my sons. Maybe I will never know what they will become or achieve as young men. But, I must believe and continue as best I know how to raise and prepare my sons for God's calling—whatever and wherever that may be.

Doris Rikkers

PASSAGE FOR THE DAY:
Daniel 1:1–21

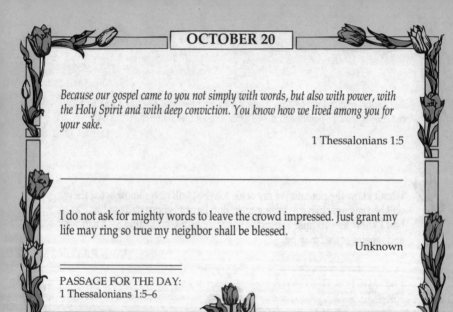

OCTOBER 20

Because our gospel came to you not simply with words, but also with power, with the Holy Spirit and with deep conviction. You know how we lived among you for your sake.

1 Thessalonians 1:5

I do not ask for mighty words to leave the crowd impressed. Just grant my life may ring so true my neighbor shall be blessed.

Unknown

PASSAGE FOR THE DAY:
1 Thessalonians 1:5–6

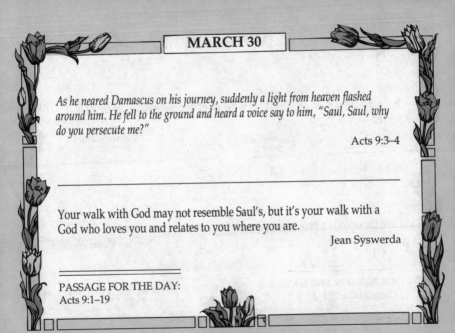

MARCH 30

As he neared Damascus on his journey, suddenly a light from heaven flashed around him. He fell to the ground and heard a voice say to him, "Saul, Saul, why do you persecute me?"

Acts 9:3–4

Your walk with God may not resemble Saul's, but it's your walk with a God who loves you and relates to you where you are.

Jean Syswerda

PASSAGE FOR THE DAY:
Acts 9:1–19

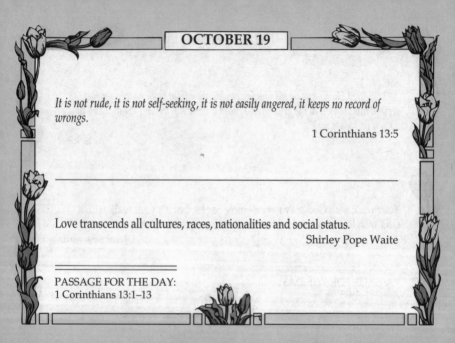

OCTOBER 19

It is not rude, it is not self-seeking, it is not easily angered, it keeps no record of wrongs.

1 Corinthians 13:5

Love transcends all cultures, races, nationalities and social status.

Shirley Pope Waite

PASSAGE FOR THE DAY:
1 Corinthians 13:1–13

For the foolishness of God is wiser than man's wisdom, and the weakness of God is stronger than man's strength.

1 Corinthians 1:25

There is sublime peace in accepting the sufficiency of God's grace by allowing him to be strong in us where we are weak.

Marie Chapian

PASSAGE FOR THE DAY:
1 Corinthians 1:25–31

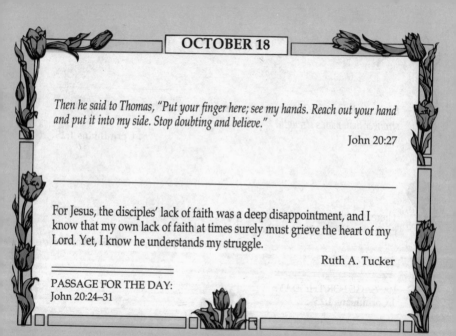

OCTOBER 18

Then he said to Thomas, "Put your finger here; see my hands. Reach out your hand and put it into my side. Stop doubting and believe."

John 20:27

For Jesus, the disciples' lack of faith was a deep disappointment, and I know that my own lack of faith at times surely must grieve the heart of my Lord. Yet, I know he understands my struggle.

Ruth A. Tucker

PASSAGE FOR THE DAY:
John 20:24–31

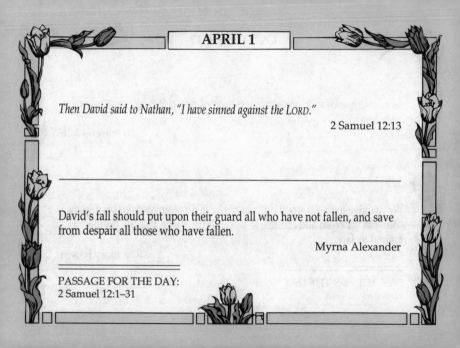

Then David said to Nathan, "I have sinned against the LORD."

2 Samuel 12:13

David's fall should put upon their guard all who have not fallen, and save from despair all those who have fallen.

Myrna Alexander

PASSAGE FOR THE DAY:
2 Samuel 12:1–31

OCTOBER 17

Because he himself suffered when he was tempted, he is able to help those who are being tempted.

Hebrews 2:18

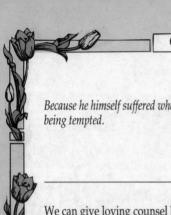

We can give loving counsel because we have contemplated the Lord Jesus Christ in his Word and are able to tackle the problems that the people around us face.

Rosemary Jensen

PASSAGE FOR THE DAY:
Hebrews 2:14–18

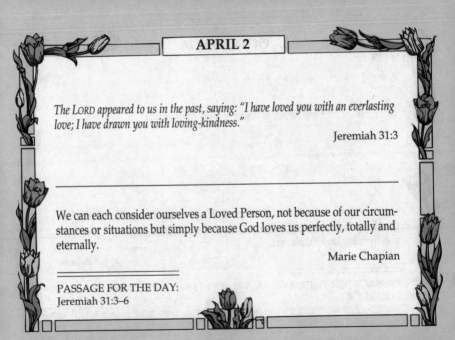

APRIL 2

The LORD appeared to us in the past, saying: "I have loved you with an everlasting love; I have drawn you with loving-kindness."

Jeremiah 31:3

We can each consider ourselves a Loved Person, not because of our circumstances or situations but simply because God loves us perfectly, totally and eternally.

Marie Chapian

PASSAGE FOR THE DAY:
Jeremiah 31:3–6

He also saw a poor widow put in two very small copper coins.

Luke 21:2

Jesus always notices the small offerings. If you've indeed cast in all you possibly can of your money, time and service, God understands. He affirms you in it. He says thank you.

Jill Briscoe

PASSAGE FOR THE DAY:
Luke 21:1–4

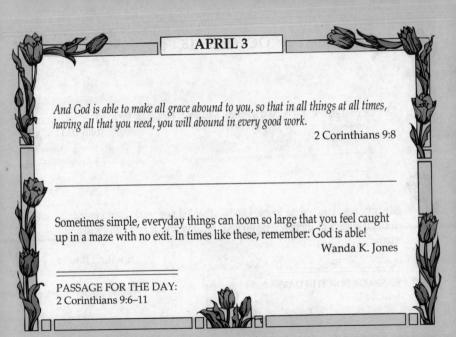

APRIL 3

And God is able to make all grace abound to you, so that in all things at all times, having all that you need, you will abound in every good work.

2 Corinthians 9:8

Sometimes simple, everyday things can loom so large that you feel caught up in a maze with no exit. In times like these, remember: God is able!

Wanda K. Jones

PASSAGE FOR THE DAY:
2 Corinthians 9:6–11

I am the good shepherd. The good shepherd lays down his life for the sheep.

John 10:11

My little one, you belong to me. I know what led you astray, but I found you. I'll always be there when you need me. My love is unconditional and eternal.

Rosalind Rinker

PASSAGE FOR THE DAY:
John 10:11–16

My soul yearns for you in the night; in the morning my spirit longs for you. When your judgments come upon the earth, the people of the world learn righteousness.

Isaiah 26:9

Celebrating each new day helps us develop the ability to be grateful for all new moments and for the God who is in each one. The discipline of celebrating each new day influences our attitude toward all of life.

Karen Burton Mains

PASSAGE FOR THE DAY:
Isaiah 25:1–12

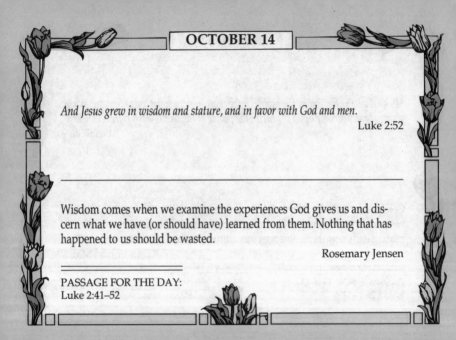

OCTOBER 14

And Jesus grew in wisdom and stature, and in favor with God and men.

Luke 2:52

Wisdom comes when we examine the experiences God gives us and discern what we have (or should have) learned from them. Nothing that has happened to us should be wasted.

Rosemary Jensen

PASSAGE FOR THE DAY:
Luke 2:41–52

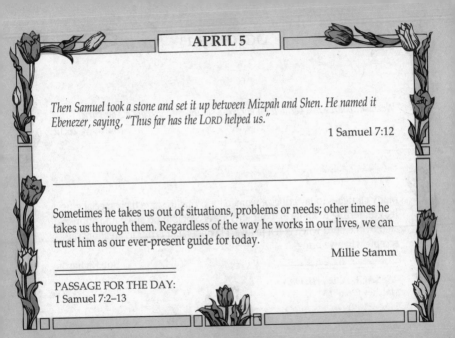

Then Samuel took a stone and set it up between Mizpah and Shen. He named it Ebenezer, saying, "Thus far has the LORD helped us."

1 Samuel 7:12

Sometimes he takes us out of situations, problems or needs; other times he takes us through them. Regardless of the way he works in our lives, we can trust him as our ever-present guide for today.

Millie Stamm

PASSAGE FOR THE DAY:
1 Samuel 7:2–13

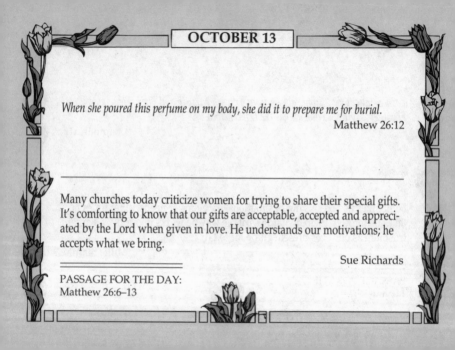

OCTOBER 13

When she poured this perfume on my body, she did it to prepare me for burial.

Matthew 26:12

Many churches today criticize women for trying to share their special gifts. It's comforting to know that our gifts are acceptable, accepted and appreciated by the Lord when given in love. He understands our motivations; he accepts what we bring.

Sue Richards

PASSAGE FOR THE DAY:
Matthew 26:6–13

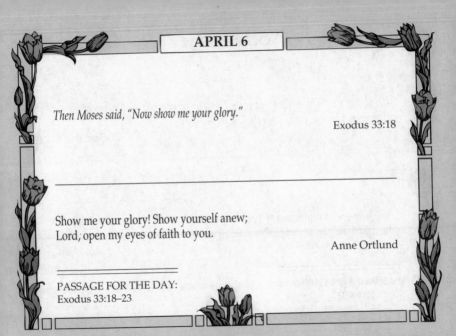

Then Moses said, "Now show me your glory."

Exodus 33:18

Show me your glory! Show yourself anew;
Lord, open my eyes of faith to you.

Anne Ortlund

PASSAGE FOR THE DAY:
Exodus 33:18–23

So he said to me, "This is the word of the Lord to Zerubbabel: 'Not by might nor by power, but by my spirit,' says the Lord Almighty."

Zechariah 4:6

Lord, help me to remember it's not by my power, nor by my might, but by your spirit that we accomplish anything worthwhile.

Nicole Hill

PASSAGE FOR THE DAY:
Zechariah 4:1–7

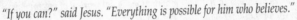

APRIL 7

"If you can?" said Jesus. "Everything is possible for him who believes."

Mark 9:23

The "everything" in this verse does not always come simply for the asking. God is ever seeking to teach us the way of faith, and in our training in the faith life there must be room for the trial of faith, the discipline of faith, the patience of faith, the courage of faith, and often many stages are passed before we realize what is the end of faith, namely, the victory of faith.

Mrs. Charles E. Cowman

PASSAGE FOR THE DAY:
Mark 9:14–21

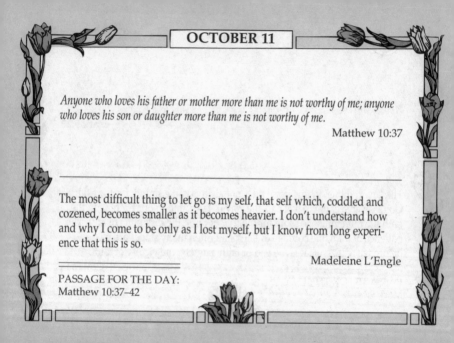

OCTOBER 11

Anyone who loves his father or mother more than me is not worthy of me; anyone who loves his son or daughter more than me is not worthy of me.

Matthew 10:37

The most difficult thing to let go is my self, that self which, coddled and cozened, becomes smaller as it becomes heavier. I don't understand how and why I come to be only as I lost myself, but I know from long experience that this is so.

Madeleine L'Engle

PASSAGE FOR THE DAY:
Matthew 10:37–42

Our fathers disciplined us for a little while as they thought best; but God disciplines us for our good, that we may share in his holiness.

Hebrews 12:10

God disciplines us for our good, that we may share in his holiness. What a difference it makes in the atmosphere of our homes if we face those calamities with an attitude of joy.

Diane Noble

PASSAGE FOR THE DAY:
Hebrews 12:1–13

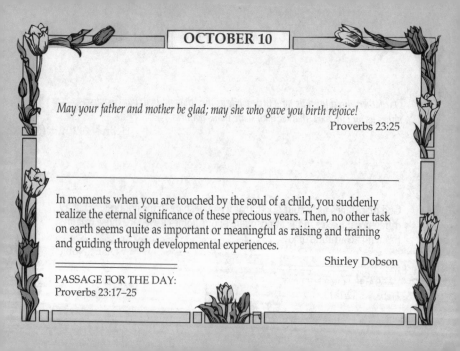

May your father and mother be glad; may she who gave you birth rejoice!

Proverbs 23:25

In moments when you are touched by the soul of a child, you suddenly realize the eternal significance of these precious years. Then, no other task on earth seems quite as important or meaningful as raising and training and guiding through developmental experiences.

Shirley Dobson

PASSAGE FOR THE DAY:
Proverbs 23:17–25

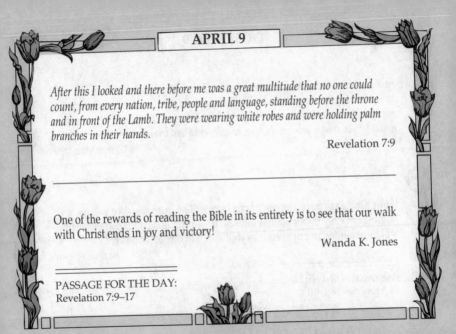

APRIL 9

After this I looked and there before me was a great multitude that no one could count, from every nation, tribe, people and language, standing before the throne and in front of the Lamb. They were wearing white robes and were holding palm branches in their hands.

Revelation 7:9

One of the rewards of reading the Bible in its entirety is to see that our walk with Christ ends in joy and victory!

Wanda K. Jones

PASSAGE FOR THE DAY:
Revelation 7:9–17

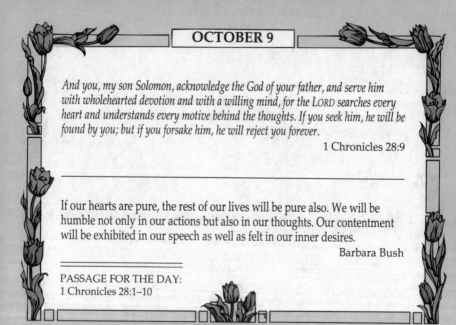

OCTOBER 9

And you, my son Solomon, acknowledge the God of your father, and serve him with wholehearted devotion and with a willing mind, for the LORD searches every heart and understands every motive behind the thoughts. If you seek him, he will be found by you; but if you forsake him, he will reject you forever.

1 Chronicles 28:9

If our hearts are pure, the rest of our lives will be pure also. We will be humble not only in our actions but also in our thoughts. Our contentment will be exhibited in our speech as well as felt in our inner desires.

Barbara Bush

PASSAGE FOR THE DAY:
1 Chronicles 28:1–10

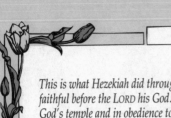

APRIL 10

This is what Hezekiah did throughout Judah, doing what was good and right and faithful before the LORD his God. In everything that he undertook in the service of God's temple and in obedience to the law and the commands, he sought his God and worked wholeheartedly. And so he prospered.

2 Chronicles 31:20–21

It dawned on me that the separation between "spiritual" activities and "worldly" activities was an artificial division. The contemplation of what God required, and the completion of the tasks he assigned, were interlocking pieces of the same abundant life he pictures for me.

Rita Schweitz

PASSAGE FOR THE DAY:
2 Chronicles 31:11–21

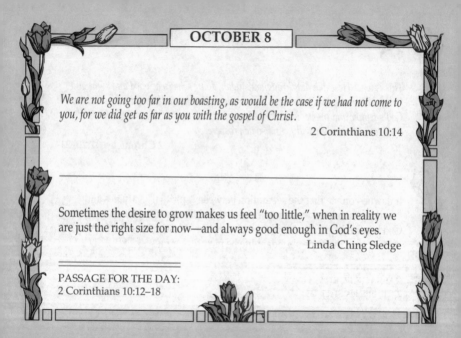

OCTOBER 8

We are not going too far in our boasting, as would be the case if we had not come to you, for we did get as far as you with the gospel of Christ.

2 Corinthians 10:14

Sometimes the desire to grow makes us feel "too little," when in reality we are just the right size for now—and always good enough in God's eyes.

Linda Ching Sledge

PASSAGE FOR THE DAY:
2 Corinthians 10:12–18

APRIL 11

She said to her mistress, "If only my master would see the prophet who is in Samaria! He would cure him of his leprosy."

2 Kings 5:3

Service for God cannot be evaluated by comparison to other people. The important thing to God is not how I measure up with others, but how I am doing with what he has given me.

June Gunden

PASSAGE FOR THE DAY:
2 Kings 5:1–15

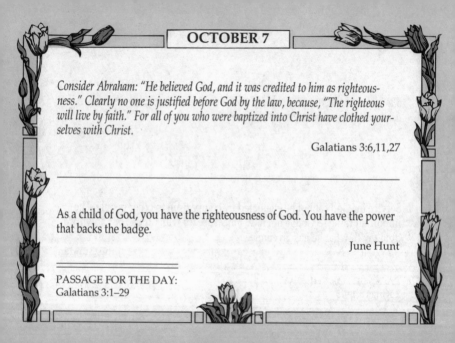

OCTOBER 7

Consider Abraham: "He believed God, and it was credited to him as righteousness." Clearly no one is justified before God by the law, because, "The righteous will live by faith." For all of you who were baptized into Christ have clothed yourselves with Christ.

Galatians 3:6,11,27

As a child of God, you have the righteousness of God. You have the power that backs the badge.

June Hunt

PASSAGE FOR THE DAY:
Galatians 3:1–29

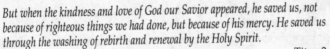

APRIL 12

But when the kindness and love of God our Savior appeared, he saved us, not because of righteous things we had done, but because of his mercy. He saved us through the washing of rebirth and renewal by the Holy Spirit.

Titus 3:4–5

Children have a wonderful ability to accept the gifts of God at face value, without feeling pride or embarrassment.

Debby Boone

PASSAGE FOR THE DAY:
Titus 3:4-8

OCTOBER 6

I tell you the truth, you will weep and mourn while the world rejoices. You will grieve, but your grief will turn to joy. So with you: Now is your time of grief, but I will see you again and you will rejoice, and no one will take away your joy.

John 16:20,22

Thank you, Father, that joy will follow my sorrows.

Sue Richards

PASSAGE FOR THE DAY:
John 16:17–24

Therefore, since we have been justified through faith, we have peace with God through our Lord Jesus Christ.

Romans 5:1

When we are at odds with God, inner peace eludes us. Becoming a Christian necessitates being made right with God, and what a difference it makes! Peace with God is enough to sing about.

Gladys M. Hunt

PASSAGE FOR THE DAY:
Romans 5:1–5

OCTOBER 5

But blessed is the man who trusts in the LORD, whose confidence is in him.

Jeremiah 17:7

Lord,
so wrap me in the
knowledge of You
that my trust is no longer in You,
but is You.

Susan L. Lenzkes

PASSAGE FOR THE DAY:
Jeremiah 17:1–10

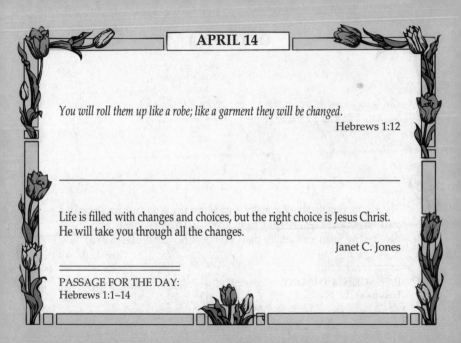

APRIL 14

You will roll them up like a robe; like a garment they will be changed.

Hebrews 1:12

Life is filled with changes and choices, but the right choice is Jesus Christ. He will take you through all the changes.

Janet C. Jones

PASSAGE FOR THE DAY:
Hebrews 1:1–14

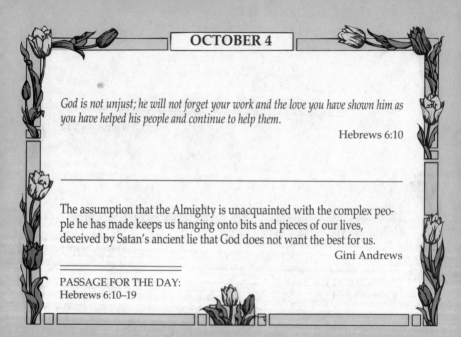

OCTOBER 4

God is not unjust; he will not forget your work and the love you have shown him as you have helped his people and continue to help them.

Hebrews 6:10

The assumption that the Almighty is unacquainted with the complex people he has made keeps us hanging onto bits and pieces of our lives, deceived by Satan's ancient lie that God does not want the best for us.

Gini Andrews

PASSAGE FOR THE DAY:
Hebrews 6:10–19

APRIL 15

When the king heard the words of the Book of the Law, he tore his robes. The king stood by the pillar and renewed the covenant in the presence of the LORD—to follow the LORD and keep his commands, regulations and decrees with all his heart and all his soul, thus confirming the words of the covenant written in this book. Then all the people pledged themselves to the covenant.

2 Kings 22:11; 23:3

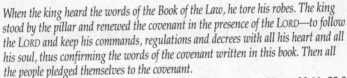

May God help us to study his "instruction manual" every day, to believe its message, and to treasure its wisdom.

June Gunden

PASSAGE FOR THE DAY:
2 Kings 22:1–23:3

Then I heard the voice of the Lord saying, "Whom shall I send? And who will go for us?" And I said, "Here am I. Send me!"

Isaiah 6:8

The Lord wants us to serve him by reaching others. Perhaps he may send you to witness to a loved one, to a neighbor, or even to a country where many have not heard of Jesus and his love.

Wanda K. Jones

PASSAGE FOR THE DAY:
Isaiah 6:1–12

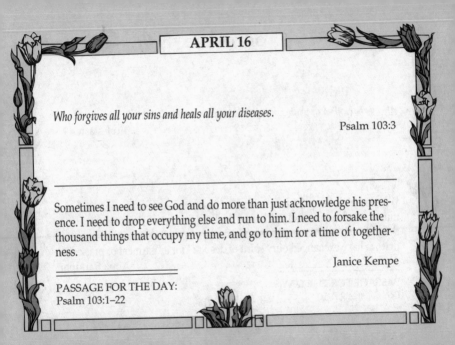

Who forgives all your sins and heals all your diseases.

Psalm 103:3

Sometimes I need to see God and do more than just acknowledge his presence. I need to drop everything else and run to him. I need to forsake the thousand things that occupy my time, and go to him for a time of togetherness.

Janice Kempe

PASSAGE FOR THE DAY:
Psalm 103:1–22

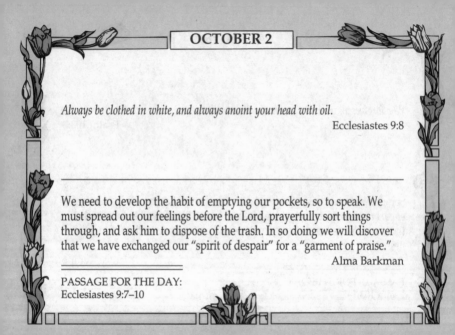

Always be clothed in white, and always anoint your head with oil.

Ecclesiastes 9:8

We need to develop the habit of emptying our pockets, so to speak. We must spread out our feelings before the Lord, prayerfully sort things through, and ask him to dispose of the trash. In so doing we will discover that we have exchanged our "spirit of despair" for a "garment of praise."

Alma Barkman

PASSAGE FOR THE DAY:
Ecclesiastes 9:7–10

APRIL 17

"The pride of your heart has deceived you, you who live in the clefts of the rocks and make your home on the heights, and who say to yourself, 'Who can bring me down to the ground?' Though you soar like the eagle and make your nest among the stars, from there I will bring you down," declares the LORD.

Obadiah 3–4

God is in control. We may think that we are in control, that we have prestige or power or success. Obadiah reminds us that we're not in control— God is. And if our pride gets in the way, God's warning is to us as it was to Edom: "I will bring you down."

Doris Rikkers

PASSAGE FOR THE DAY:
Obadiah 1–21

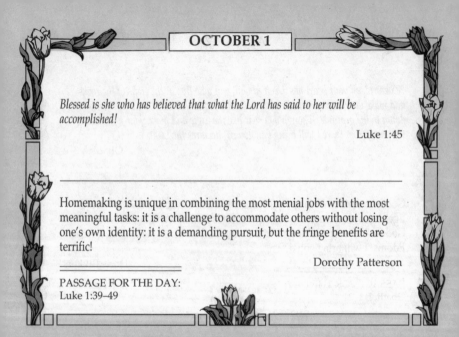

Blessed is she who has believed that what the Lord has said to her will be accomplished!

Luke 1:45

Homemaking is unique in combining the most menial jobs with the most meaningful tasks: it is a challenge to accommodate others without losing one's own identity: it is a demanding pursuit, but the fringe benefits are terrific!

Dorothy Patterson

PASSAGE FOR THE DAY:
Luke 1:39–49

Now the serpent was more crafty than any of the wild animals the LORD God had made. He said to the woman, "Did God really say, 'You must not eat from any tree in the garden'?"

Genesis 3:1

Satan is very clever. Always his strategy is to confuse reality, to make evil seem good.

Gladys M. Hunt

PASSAGE FOR THE DAY:
Genesis 3:1–6

Circumcise your hearts, therefore, and do not be stiff-necked any longer.

Deuteronomy 10:16

How often I have thought that if I could give just one gift to my children—besides a heart for God—it would be the golden gift of flexibility.

Susan L. Lenzkes

PASSAGE FOR THE DAY:
Deuteronomy 10:12–22

APRIL 19

Now the Bereans were of more noble character than the Thessalonians, for they received the message with great eagerness and examined the Scriptures every day to see if what Paul said was true.

Acts 17:11

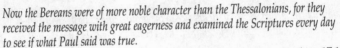

We have many Bibles in our home, but one in particular is my sentimental favorite. This book, which I handle with such careless, casual ease and freedom, would not be mine if it were not for those women (and men) who boldly claimed their right to have the Word of God—a right they paid for with their own blood.

Elizabeth Larson

PASSAGE FOR THE DAY:
Acts 17:10–15

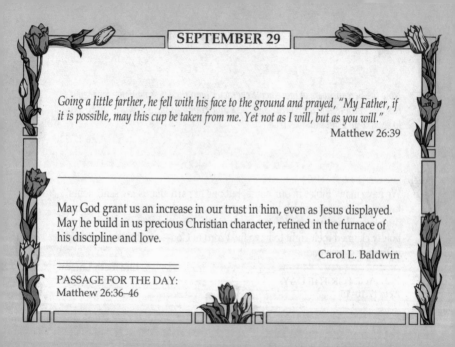

Going a little farther, he fell with his face to the ground and prayed, "My Father, if it is possible, may this cup be taken from me. Yet not as I will, but as you will."

Matthew 26:39

May God grant us an increase in our trust in him, even as Jesus displayed. May he build in us precious Christian character, refined in the furnace of his discipline and love.

Carol L. Baldwin

PASSAGE FOR THE DAY:
Matthew 26:36–46

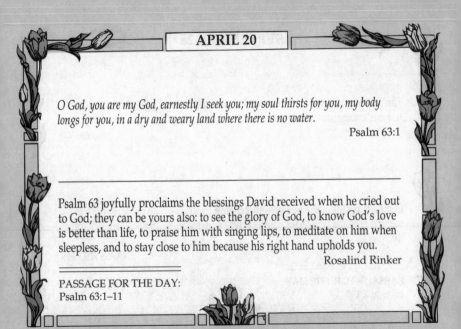

O God, you are my God, earnestly I seek you; my soul thirsts for you, my body longs for you, in a dry and weary land where there is no water.

Psalm 63:1

Psalm 63 joyfully proclaims the blessings David received when he cried out to God; they can be yours also: to see the glory of God, to know God's love is better than life, to praise him with singing lips, to meditate on him when sleepless, and to stay close to him because his right hand upholds you.

Rosalind Rinker

PASSAGE FOR THE DAY:
Psalm 63:1–11

This is what I covenanted with you when you came out of Egypt. And my Spirit remains among you. Do not fear.

Haggai 2:5

Our God is still in the business of keeping promises. The promise of this verse is true for you today just as it was true for those exiled Jews in captivity.

Doris Rikkers

PASSAGE FOR THE DAY:
Haggai 2:1–9

APRIL 21

And observe what the LORD your God requires: Walk in his ways, and keep his decrees and commands, his laws and requirements, as written in the Law of Moses, so that you may prosper in all you do and wherever you go.

1 Kings 2:3

God is powerful. Through the strength and wisdom of his Spirit we have had opportunity to demonstrate to our children in many practical ways the same important reality of David's charge to his son.

Myrna Alexander

PASSAGE FOR THE DAY:
1 Kings 2:1–12

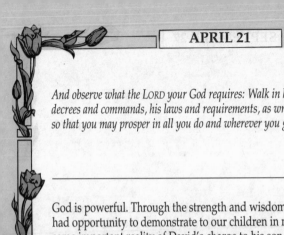

When I am afraid, I will trust in you.

Psalm 56:3

We work hard to get ahead, do well and avoid pain. But our efforts may fail. Only the compassion of the Lord will never fail. His faithfulness is monumental, majestic, true and permanently dependable.

Marie Chapian

PASSAGE FOR THE DAY:
Psalm 56:3–4

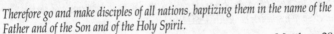

APRIL 22

Therefore go and make disciples of all nations, baptizing them in the name of the Father and of the Son and of the Holy Spirit.

Matthew 28:19

Christians should be more like dandelions. Our sunny yellow faces should be a reminder that simple faith has deep roots that are impossible to dislodge. Our vast number would show the world that even though we are not fancy or pampered we are evident everywhere, even in the best neighborhoods.

Janice Kempe

PASSAGE FOR THE DAY:
Matthew 28:16–20

SEPTEMBER 26

He tends his flock like a shepherd: He gathers the lambs in his arms and carries them close to his heart; he gently leads those that have young.

Isaiah 40:1

As I look back on the painful experience of my childhood, I am overwhelmed with gratitude to God for answering my early prayers. I had no status, no special abilities, no money to contribute. Yet the Creator of the universe entered my little room and communed with me about the difficulties I was experiencing. It was awesome to realize that he loved me just as I was, and my pain became his pain. What a magnificent God we serve!

Shirley Dobson

PASSAGE FOR THE DAY:
Isaiah 40:1–44

And the God of all grace, who called you to his eternal glory in Christ, after you have suffered a little while, will himself restore you and make you strong, firm and steadfast.

1 Peter 5:10

I am reminded that just like the water lilies in Monet's masterpiece, God keeps the leaves and petals afloat through the muck, wind and rain that are part of the storms of life. Water gardens survive April showers and worse, and I will too, by God's help and grace.

Beth Donigan Seversen

PASSAGE FOR THE DAY:
1 Peter 5:1–11

Commit to the LORD whatever you do, and your plans will succeed.

Proverbs 16:3

Surrender your blunders to the Lord. He can use them to make the pattern of your life more beautiful.

Corrie ten Boom

PASSAGE FOR THE DAY:
Proverbs 16:1–9

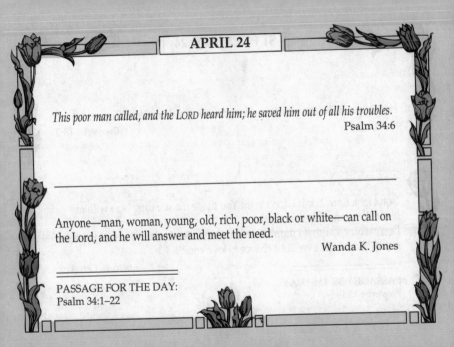

APRIL 24

*This poor man called, and the L*ORD *heard him; he saved him out of all his troubles.*
Psalm 34:6

Anyone—man, woman, young, old, rich, poor, black or white—can call on the Lord, and he will answer and meet the need.

Wanda K. Jones

PASSAGE FOR THE DAY:
Psalm 34:1–22

He who guards his lips guards his life, but he who speaks rashly will come to ruin.

Proverbs 13:3

Don't look now, Lord! I don't want You to see me standing here with my big foot crammed in my mouth.

Don't worry, child. If I didn't love you just as much with your foot in your mouth, I'd hardly ever get a chance to love you.

Susan L. Lenzkes

PASSAGE FOR THE DAY:
Proverbs 13:1–5

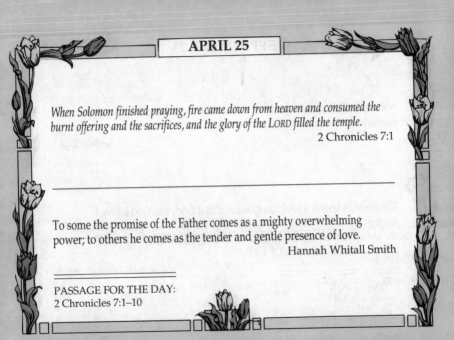

When Solomon finished praying, fire came down from heaven and consumed the burnt offering and the sacrifices, and the glory of the LORD filled the temple.

2 Chronicles 7:1

To some the promise of the Father comes as a mighty overwhelming power; to others he comes as the tender and gentle presence of love.

Hannah Whitall Smith

PASSAGE FOR THE DAY:
2 Chronicles 7:1–10

SEPTEMBER 23

Not one of all the LORD's good promises to the house of Israel failed; every one was fulfilled.

Joshua 21:45

The greatest lesson a soul has to learn is that God, and God alone, is enough for all its needs. This is the lesson that all God's dealings with us are meant to teach, and this is the crowning discovery of our entire Christian life. GOD IS ENOUGH!

Hannah Whitall Smith

PASSAGE FOR THE DAY:
Joshua 21:43–45

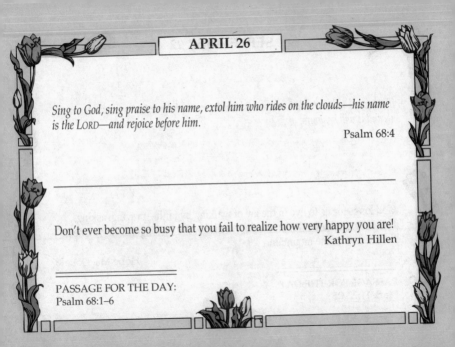

APRIL 26

Sing to God, sing praise to his name, extol him who rides on the clouds—his name is the LORD—and rejoice before him.

Psalm 68:4

Don't ever become so busy that you fail to realize how very happy you are!

Kathryn Hillen

PASSAGE FOR THE DAY:
Psalm 68:1–6

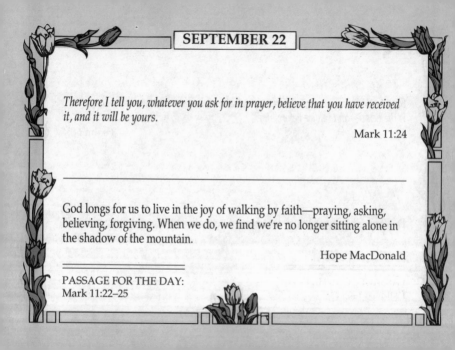

SEPTEMBER 22

Therefore I tell you, whatever you ask for in prayer, believe that you have received it, and it will be yours.

Mark 11:24

God longs for us to live in the joy of walking by faith—praying, asking, believing, forgiving. When we do, we find we're no longer sitting alone in the shadow of the mountain.

Hope MacDonald

PASSAGE FOR THE DAY:
Mark 11:22–25

APRIL 27

Say to Aaron: "For the generations to come none of your descendants who has a defect may come near to offer the food of his God."

Leviticus 21:17

As part of "royal priesthood," God welcomes us into his presence, accepting us no matter how "disfigured or deformed" we are. But when we come before him in worship, we need to make certain that we have been washed in Jesus' blood and our hearts are clean, harboring no blemish of pride or defect of impurity.

Joni Eareckson Tada

PASSAGE FOR THE DAY:
Leviticus 21:1–24

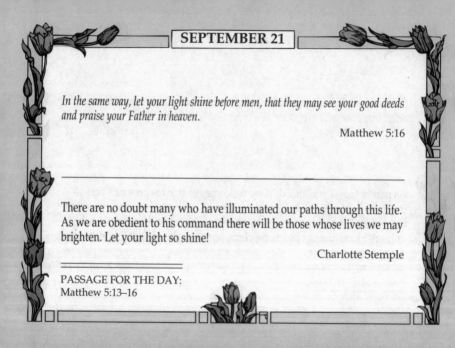

SEPTEMBER 21

In the same way, let your light shine before men, that they may see your good deeds and praise your Father in heaven.

Matthew 5:16

There are no doubt many who have illuminated our paths through this life. As we are obedient to his command there will be those whose lives we may brighten. Let your light so shine!

Charlotte Stemple

PASSAGE FOR THE DAY:
Matthew 5:13–16

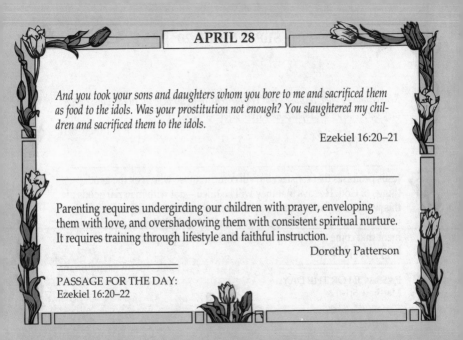

APRIL 28

And you took your sons and daughters whom you bore to me and sacrificed them as food to the idols. Was your prostitution not enough? You slaughtered my children and sacrificed them to the idols.

Ezekiel 16:20–21

Parenting requires undergirding our children with prayer, enveloping them with love, and overshadowing them with consistent spiritual nurture. It requires training through lifestyle and faithful instruction.

Dorothy Patterson

PASSAGE FOR THE DAY:
Ezekiel 16:20–22

Rejoice and be glad, because great is your reward in heaven, for in the same way they persecuted the prophets who before you.

Matthew 5:12

Jesus promises that satisfaction will come to those who seek the good things of God. He says that they will be filled—not with material goods of this world, not with an easy way of life, not with something of limited value that can be taken away from them . . . but with the joy and contentment that come from doing God's will. The filled people are the truly happy people in life.

Colleen Townsend Evans

PASSAGE FOR THE DAY:
Matthew 5:1–12

All the believers were one in heart and mind. No one claimed that any of his possessions was his own, but they shared everything they had.

Acts 4:32

In Christ there is no East or West, in Him no South or North; But one great fellowship of love throughout the whole wide earth.

Linda Ching Sledge

PASSAGE FOR THE DAY:
Acts 4:23–35

Moreover, when God gives any man wealth and possessions, and enables him to enjoy them, to accept his lot and be happy in his work—this is a gift of God.

Ecclesiastes 5:19

A retired schoolteacher who volunteered in a city mission was asked how she could go on day after day. "I don't ever have time to think about it," she replied. She had accepted her lot: God wanted her in the mission. She was happy in her work.

Jean Shaw

PASSAGE FOR THE DAY:
Ecclesiastes 5:18–20

"But let him who boasts boast about this: that he understands and knows me, that I am the LORD, who exercises kindness, justice and righteousness on earth, for in these I delight," declares the LORD.

Jeremiah 9:24

The Lord's gentle voice reminds me that what is important is not what I am or can attain, but who I know him to be in and through me. A light goes on in my little brain, priorities take shape, and the weight of this backward world is lifted off my shoulders.

Debby Boone

PASSAGE FOR THE DAY:
Jeremiah 9:23–24

SEPTEMBER 18

Trust in the LORD with all your heart and lean not on your own understanding; in all your ways acknowledge him, and he will make your paths straight.

Proverbs 3:5–6

Let go completely. Trust. Live with it all in an open hand before God. Jesus promises he will work it all out. I do believe for you, always . . . a new sunrise.

Ann Kiemel Anderson

PASSAGE FOR THE DAY:
Proverbs 3:1–8

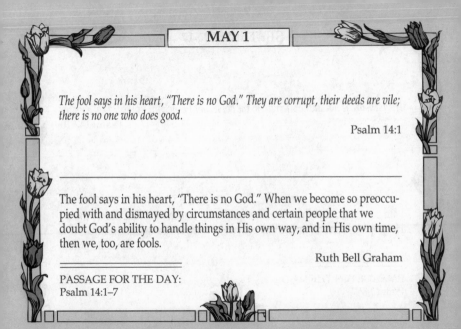

MAY 1

The fool says in his heart, "There is no God." They are corrupt, their deeds are vile; there is no one who does good.

Psalm 14:1

The fool says in his heart, "There is no God." When we become so preoccupied with and dismayed by circumstances and certain people that we doubt God's ability to handle things in His own way, and in His own time, then we, too, are fools.

Ruth Bell Graham

PASSAGE FOR THE DAY:
Psalm 14:1–7

His pleasure is not in the strength of the horse, nor his delight in the legs of a man.

Psalm 147:10

I am convinced that there is no insignificant verse in the Bible. Surely the Holy Spirit has used them all to convict, correct, encourage and edify.

Debbie Smith

PASSAGE FOR THE DAY:
Psalm 147:7–11

Do not support that I have come to bring peace to the earth. I did not come to bring peace, but a sword.

Matthew 10:34

Jesus knew the coming of the gospel would bring division within families—it brought it in his own. The gospel will bring reactions and responses—even from within our families. Disciples must be ready for them.

Jill Briscoe

PASSAGE FOR THE DAY:
Matthew 10:32–42

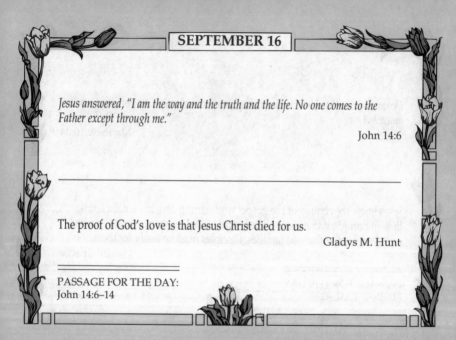

Jesus answered, "I am the way and the truth and the life. No one comes to the Father except through me."

John 14:6

The proof of God's love is that Jesus Christ died for us.

Gladys M. Hunt

PASSAGE FOR THE DAY:
John 14:6–14

MAY 3

This righteousness from God comes through faith in Jesus Christ to all who believe. There is no difference.

Romans 3:22

In justifying us, God takes care of our sin—and then does something even greater—he gives us the righteousness of Jesus Christ. He doesn't change his standard in order to include us. He changes us to fit the standard.

Gladys M. Hunt

PASSAGE FOR THE DAY:
Romans 3:9–27

SEPTEMBER 15

You warned them to return to your law, but they became arrogant and disobeyed your commands. They sinned against your ordinances, by which a man will live if he obeys them. Stubbornly they turned their backs on you, became stiff-necked and refused to listen.

Nehemiah 9:29

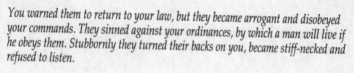

When our rest changed to unrest, we must return to God and appeal to his forgiveness and compassion. This is corrective living. Preventative living is obeying God's Word—the Bible—in order that we take the right road from the very beginning.

Gien Karssen

PASSAGE FOR THE DAY:
Nehemiah 9:28–37

May the Lord direct your hearts into God's love and Christ's perseverance. Now may the Lord of peace himself give you peace at all times and in every way. The Lord be with all of you.

2 Thessalonians 3:5,16

Peace must be practical and practiced! We best begin each new day with God, reading his Word and praying. Then we can think back to this quiet time throughout the day to claim his peace when unrest and discord are knocking at our door.

Gien Karssen

PASSAGE FOR THE DAY:
2 Thessalonians 3:1–18

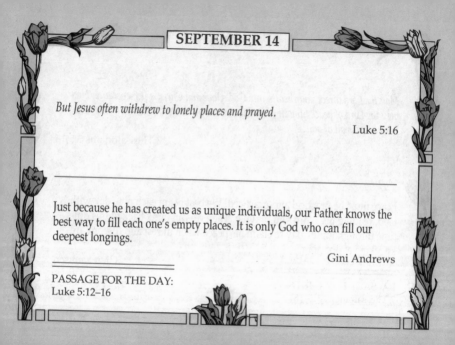

SEPTEMBER 14

But Jesus often withdrew to lonely places and prayed.

Luke 5:16

Just because he has created us as unique individuals, our Father knows the best way to fill each one's empty places. It is only God who can fill our deepest longings.

Gini Andrews

PASSAGE FOR THE DAY:
Luke 5:12–16

He himself went a day's journey into the desert. He came to a broom tree, sat down under it and prayed that he might die. "I have had enough, LORD," he said. "Take my life; I am no better than my ancestors."

1 Kings 19:4

Follow the Lord's prescription for discouragement:
1) Get enough rest. 2) Eat healthy foods on a regular basis. 3) Spend some quiet time with yourself and the Lord. 4) Now go.

Jean E. Syswerda

PASSAGE FOR THE DAY:
1 Kings 18:16–19:18

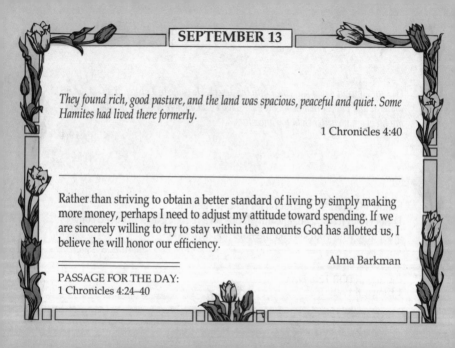

They found rich, good pasture, and the land was spacious, peaceful and quiet. Some Hamites had lived there formerly.

1 Chronicles 4:40

Rather than striving to obtain a better standard of living by simply making more money, perhaps I need to adjust my attitude toward spending. If we are sincerely willing to try to stay within the amounts God has allotted us, I believe he will honor our efficiency.

Alma Barkman

PASSAGE FOR THE DAY:
1 Chronicles 4:24–40

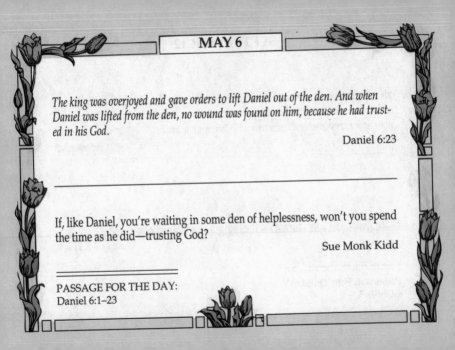

The king was overjoyed and gave orders to lift Daniel out of the den. And when Daniel was lifted from the den, no wound was found on him, because he had trusted in his God.

Daniel 6:23

If, like Daniel, you're waiting in some den of helplessness, won't you spend the time as he did—trusting God?

Sue Monk Kidd

PASSAGE FOR THE DAY:
Daniel 6:1–23

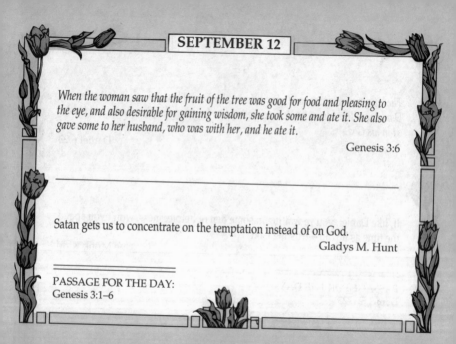

SEPTEMBER 12

When the woman saw that the fruit of the tree was good for food and pleasing to the eye, and also desirable for gaining wisdom, she took some and ate it. She also gave some to her husband, who was with her, and he ate it.

Genesis 3:6

Satan gets us to concentrate on the temptation instead of on God.

Gladys M. Hunt

PASSAGE FOR THE DAY:
Genesis 3:1–6

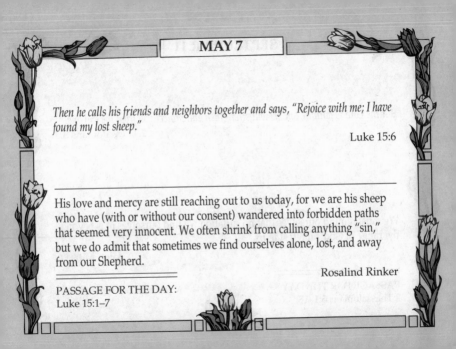

MAY 7

Then he calls his friends and neighbors together and says, "Rejoice with me; I have found my lost sheep."

Luke 15:6

His love and mercy are still reaching out to us today, for we are his sheep who have (with or without our consent) wandered into forbidden paths that seemed very innocent. We often shrink from calling anything "sin," but we do admit that sometimes we find ourselves alone, lost, and away from our Shepherd.

Rosalind Rinker

PASSAGE FOR THE DAY:
Luke 15:1–7

But the Lord is faithful, and he will strengthen and protect you from the evil one.

2 Thessalonians 3:3

We must remind ourselves that no situation we find ourselves in is beyond the range of God's interest in us.

Gien Karssen

PASSAGE FOR THE DAY:
2 Thessalonians 3:1–18

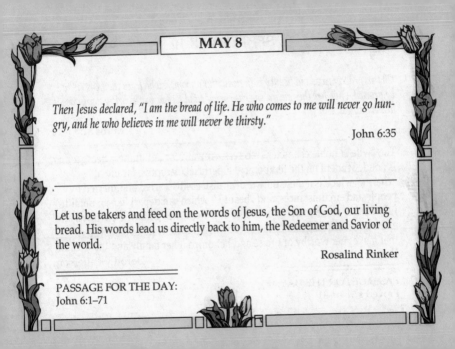

Then Jesus declared, "I am the bread of life. He who comes to me will never go hungry, and he who believes in me will never be thirsty."

John 6:35

Let us be takers and feed on the words of Jesus, the Son of God, our living bread. His words lead us directly back to him, the Redeemer and Savior of the world.

Rosalind Rinker

PASSAGE FOR THE DAY:
John 6:1–71

SEPTEMBER 10

Charm is deceptive, and beauty is fleeting; but a woman who fears the LORD is to be praised. Give her the reward she has earned, and let her works bring her praise at the city gate.

Proverbs 31:30–31

The "wife of noble character" receives a reward for faithfulness because she is not dependent on the temporary, superficial, deceptive facade of "charm," which is a mere outward varnish easily scarred and marred by people and circumstances, and "beauty," which can depart like an unfaithful friend to make room for wrinkles and blemishes. Rather she crowns an enduring, satisfying fear of the Lord with a reverent and obedient spirit that makes her worthy of praise and honor from her family and the Creator himself.

Dorothy Patterson

PASSAGE FOR THE DAY:
Proverbs 31:10–31

Your attitude should be the same as that of Christ Jesus.

Philippians 2:5

I still struggle with the problem of controlling my mind and my tongue. I ask the Lord to forgive me and to give me more and more the mind and heart and attitude of Christ.

Gigi Graham Tchividjian

PASSAGE FOR THE DAY:
Philippians 2:1–5

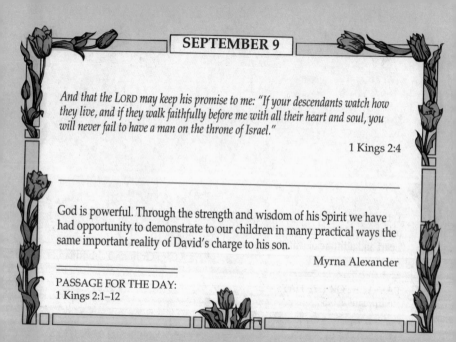

And that the LORD may keep his promise to me: "If your descendants watch how they live, and if they walk faithfully before me with all their heart and soul, you will never fail to have a man on the throne of Israel."

1 Kings 2:4

God is powerful. Through the strength and wisdom of his Spirit we have had opportunity to demonstrate to our children in many practical ways the same important reality of David's charge to his son.

Myrna Alexander

PASSAGE FOR THE DAY:
1 Kings 2:1–12

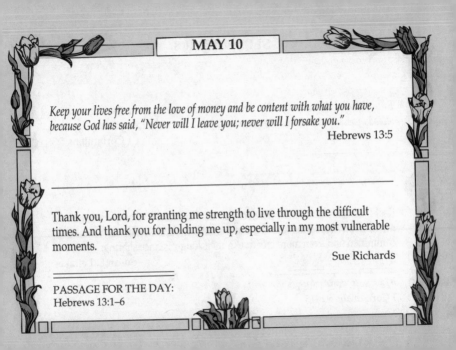

MAY 10

Keep your lives free from the love of money and be content with what you have, because God has said, "Never will I leave you; never will I forsake you."

Hebrews 13:5

Thank you, Lord, for granting me strength to live through the difficult times. And thank you for holding me up, especially in my most vulnerable moments.

Sue Richards

PASSAGE FOR THE DAY:
Hebrews 13:1–6

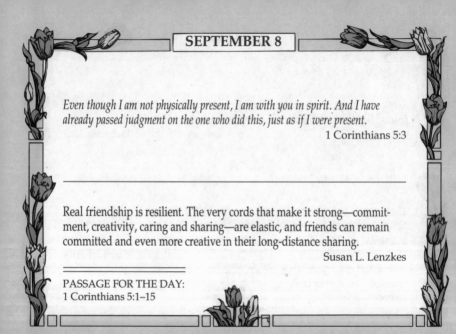

SEPTEMBER 8

Even though I am not physically present, I am with you in spirit. And I have already passed judgment on the one who did this, just as if I were present.

1 Corinthians 5:3

Real friendship is resilient. The very cords that make it strong—commitment, creativity, caring and sharing—are elastic, and friends can remain committed and even more creative in their long-distance sharing.

Susan L. Lenzkes

PASSAGE FOR THE DAY:
1 Corinthians 5:1–15

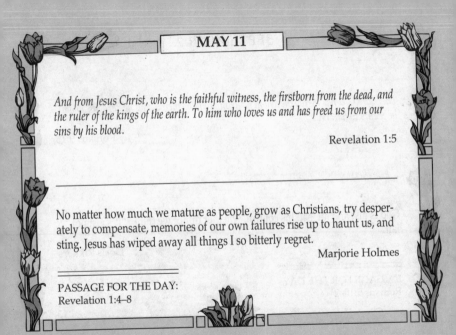

MAY 11

And from Jesus Christ, who is the faithful witness, the firstborn from the dead, and the ruler of the kings of the earth. To him who loves us and has freed us from our sins by his blood.

Revelation 1:5

No matter how much we mature as people, grow as Christians, try desperately to compensate, memories of our own failures rise up to haunt us, and sting. Jesus has wiped away all things I so bitterly regret.

Marjorie Holmes

PASSAGE FOR THE DAY:
Revelation 1:4–8

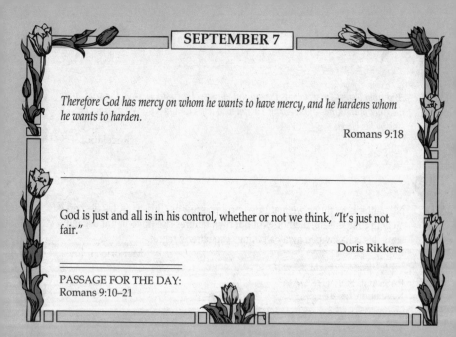

SEPTEMBER 7

Therefore God has mercy on whom he wants to have mercy, and he hardens whom he wants to harden.

Romans 9:18

God is just and all is in his control, whether or not we think, "It's just not fair."

Doris Rikkers

PASSAGE FOR THE DAY:
Romans 9:10–21

MAY 12

And to provide for those who grieve in Zion—to bestow on them a crown of beauty instead of ashes, the oil of gladness instead of mourning, and a garment of praise instead of a spirit of despair. They will be called oaks of righteousness, a planting of the LORD for the display of his splendor.

Isaiah 61:3

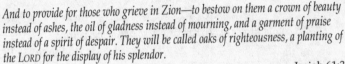

I am convinced that God has built into all of us, in varying degrees, the capacity for an appreciation of beauty, and has even allowed us the privilege of participating in the creation of beautiful things and beautiful places. I think it may be one way God brings healing to our brokenness, and a way that we can contribute toward bringing wholeness to our fallen world.

Mary Jane Worden

PASSAGE FOR THE DAY:
Isaiah 61:1–6

The LORD is near to all who call on him, to all who call on him in truth.

Psalm 145:18

Great is the Lord, he is holy and just; By his power we trust in his love.

Debbie Smith

PASSAGE FOR THE DAY:
Psalm 145:1–21

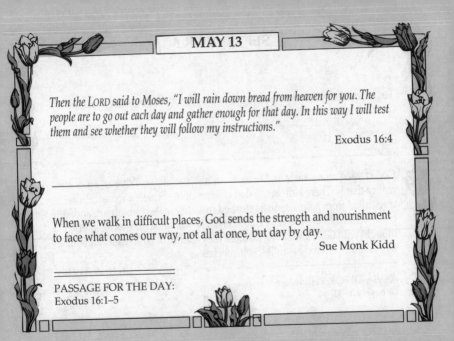

MAY 13

Then the LORD said to Moses, "I will rain down bread from heaven for you. The people are to go out each day and gather enough for that day. In this way I will test them and see whether they will follow my instructions."

Exodus 16:4

When we walk in difficult places, God sends the strength and nourishment to face what comes our way, not all at once, but day by day.

Sue Monk Kidd

PASSAGE FOR THE DAY:
Exodus 16:1–5

So God created man in his own image, in the image of God he created him; male and female he created them.

Genesis 1:27

God created man—male and female—in his own image. What an awesome reality that is. There I am in the first chapter of the Bible—a woman—distinguished from animals, distinguished from my male counterpart, and literally created in the image of God. Certainly womanhood was no afterthought with God, and it was through the creation of both male and female that God has offered his fullest self-revelation.

Ruth A. Tucker

PASSAGE FOR THE DAY:
Genesis 1:1–31

Love the LORD your God with all your heart and with all your soul and with all your strength.

Deuteronomy 6:5

I made my choice and my children have been my high priority. We decided to live with less financial security, and we have not forgotten that the Lord brought us through those times, out of financial bondage.

Beverly LaHaye

PASSAGE FOR THE DAY:
Deuteronomy 6:5–12

For you were once darkness, but now you are light in the Lord. Live as children of light.

Ephesians 5:8

When you feel the frustration of wandering in the dark, know that the Lord has already provided the perfect guide for your life.

June Hunt

PASSAGE FOR THE DAY:
Ephesians 5:8–14

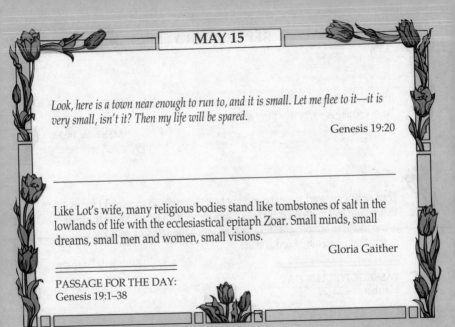

MAY 15

Look, here is a town near enough to run to, and it is small. Let me flee to it—it is very small, isn't it? Then my life will be spared.

Genesis 19:20

Like Lot's wife, many religious bodies stand like tombstones of salt in the lowlands of life with the ecclesiastical epitaph Zoar. Small minds, small dreams, small men and women, small visions.

Gloria Gaither

PASSAGE FOR THE DAY:
Genesis 19:1–38

After he had dismissed them, he went up on a mountainside by himself to pray. When evening came, he was there alone.

Matthew 14:23

Lord, when my soul is weary and my heart is tired and sore, and I have that failing feeling that I can't take it any more; then let me know the freshening found in simple, childlike prayer, when the kneeling soul knows surely that a listening Lord is there.

Ruth Bell Graham

PASSAGE FOR THE DAY:
Matthew 14:22–23

MAY 16

Then Nehemiah the governor, Ezra the priest and scribe, and the Levites who were instructing the people said to them all, "This day is sacred to the LORD your God. Do not mourn or weep." For all the people had been weeping as they listened to the words of the Law. Nehemiah said, "Go and enjoy choice food and sweet drinks, and send some to those who have nothing prepared. This day is sacred to our Lord. Do not grieve, for the joy of the LORD is your strength."

Nehemiah 8:9–10

I am grateful, God, for tears. For the ability to cry. And thank you, Lord, for laughter. Just as you saved tears for human beings, you blessed us alone with laughter. And surely this too is a clue to your very nature. A nature akin to our own.

Marjorie Holmes

PASSAGE FOR THE DAY:
Nehemiah 8:1–10

SEPTEMBER 2

I will repay you for the years the locusts have eaten—the great locust and the young locust, the other locust and the locust swarm—my great army that I sent among you.

Joel 2:25

It is good to regret missed opportunities, but quite wrong to be miserable about them. Lord Jesus, I give my "if onlies" to you. Make me a faithful laborer here and now.

Corrie ten Boom

PASSAGE FOR THE DAY:
Joel 2:18–27

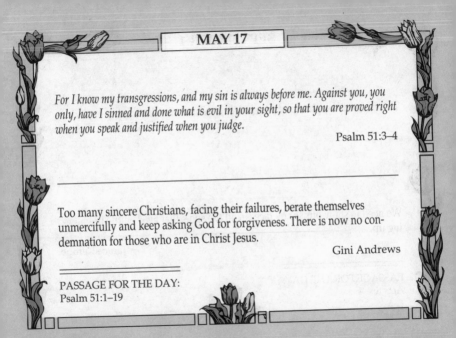

MAY 17

For I know my transgressions, and my sin is always before me. Against you, you only, have I sinned and done what is evil in your sight, so that you are proved right when you speak and justified when you judge.

Psalm 51:3–4

Too many sincere Christians, facing their failures, berate themselves unmercifully and keep asking God for forgiveness. There is now no condemnation for those who are in Christ Jesus.

Gini Andrews

PASSAGE FOR THE DAY:
Psalm 51:1–19

Those who had been scattered preached the word wherever they went.

Acts 8:4

We need to show our sunny faces in all the spots that need a little brightening up.

Janice Kempe

PASSAGE FOR THE DAY:
Acts 8:1–4

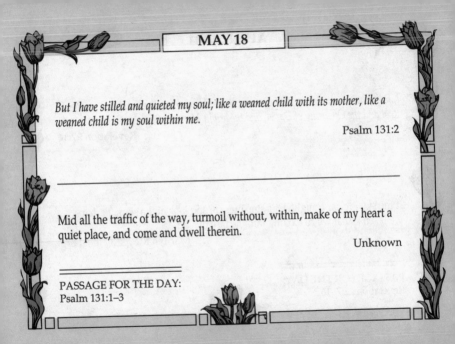

MAY 18

But I have stilled and quieted my soul; like a weaned child with its mother, like a weaned child is my soul within me.

Psalm 131:2

Mid all the traffic of the way, turmoil without, within, make of my heart a quiet place, and come and dwell therein.

Unknown

PASSAGE FOR THE DAY:
Psalm 131:1–3

AUGUST 31

I, Jesus, have sent my angel to give you this testimony for the churches. I am the Root and the Offspring of David, and the bright Morning Star.

Revelation 22:16

If the sky is clear tonight, let's step outside and look at the stars. Perhaps, we'll sense that we're looking into the face of God.

Marilyn Morgan Helleberg

PASSAGE FOR THE DAY:
Revelation 22:7–16

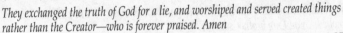

MAY 19

*They exchanged the truth of God for a lie, and worshiped and served created things
rather than the Creator—who is forever praised. Amen*

Romans 1:25

It is our responsibility and joy to look at babies and delight in their perfectly formed tiny hands and feet—and then worship the one who created those parts with infinite wisdom, care and direction.

Carol L. Baldwin

PASSAGE FOR THE DAY:
Romans 1:18–25

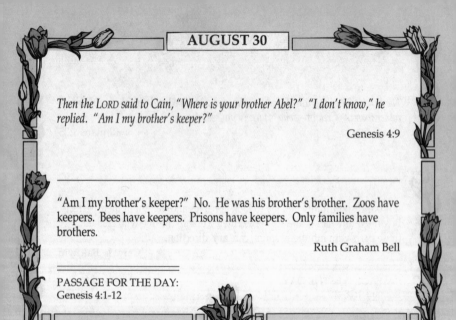

Then the LORD *said to Cain, "Where is your brother Abel?" "I don't know," he replied. "Am I my brother's keeper?"*

Genesis 4:9

"Am I my brother's keeper?" No. He was his brother's brother. Zoos have keepers. Bees have keepers. Prisons have keepers. Only families have brothers.

Ruth Graham Bell

PASSAGE FOR THE DAY:
Genesis 4:1-12

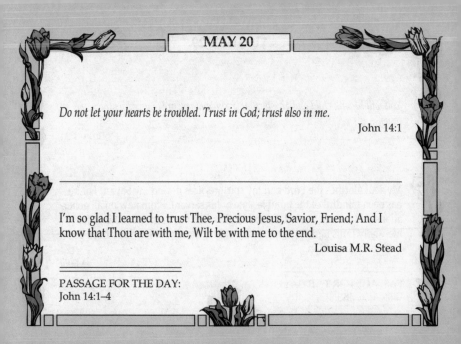

Do not let your hearts be troubled. Trust in God; trust also in me.

John 14:1

I'm so glad I learned to trust Thee, Precious Jesus, Savior, Friend; And I know that Thou are with me, Wilt be with me to the end.

Louisa M.R. Stead

PASSAGE FOR THE DAY:
John 14:1–4

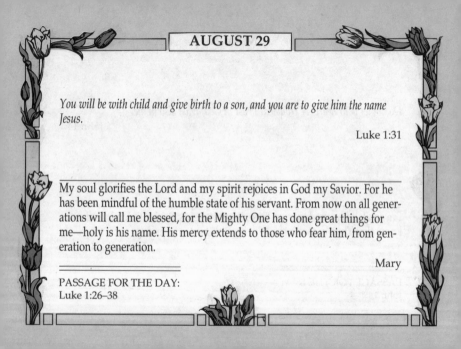

You will be with child and give birth to a son, and you are to give him the name Jesus.

Luke 1:31

My soul glorifies the Lord and my spirit rejoices in God my Savior. For he has been mindful of the humble state of his servant. From now on all generations will call me blessed, for the Mighty One has done great things for me—holy is his name. His mercy extends to those who fear him, from generation to generation.

Mary

PASSAGE FOR THE DAY:
Luke 1:26–38

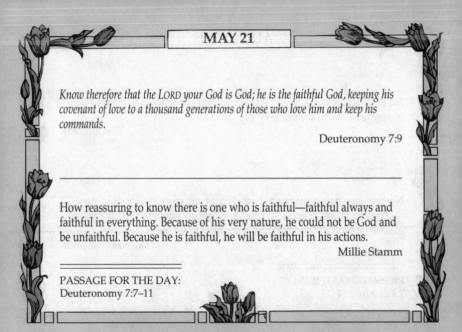

Know therefore that the LORD your God is God; he is the faithful God, keeping his covenant of love to a thousand generations of those who love him and keep his commands.

Deuteronomy 7:9

How reassuring to know there is one who is faithful—faithful always and faithful in everything. Because of his very nature, he could not be God and be unfaithful. Because he is faithful, he will be faithful in his actions.

Millie Stamm

PASSAGE FOR THE DAY:
Deuteronomy 7:7–11

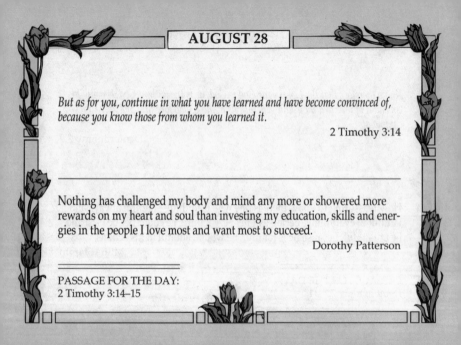

AUGUST 28

But as for you, continue in what you have learned and have become convinced of, because you know those from whom you learned it.

2 Timothy 3:14

Nothing has challenged my body and mind any more or showered more rewards on my heart and soul than investing my education, skills and energies in the people I love most and want most to succeed.

Dorothy Patterson

PASSAGE FOR THE DAY:
2 Timothy 3:14–15

MAY 22

But if serving the LORD seems undesirable to you, then choose for yourselves this day whom you will serve, whether the gods your forefather served beyond the River, or the gods of the Amorites, in whose land you are living. But as for me and my household, we will serve the LORD.

Joshua 24:15

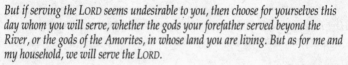

A friend's father cut out of wood those words of Joshua. Today they stretch across the front of our fireplace mantel—a testimony to our friends and a reminder to us: As for me and my household, we will serve the Lord.

Jean E. Syswerda

PASSAGE FOR THE DAY:
Joshua 24:1–27

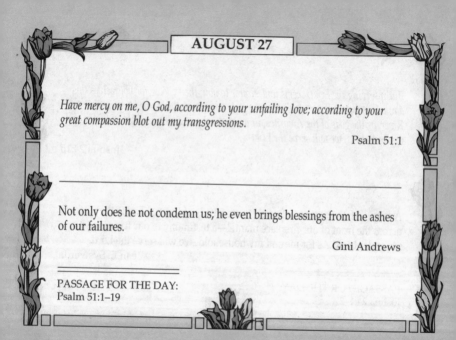

AUGUST 27

Have mercy on me, O God, according to your unfailing love; according to your great compassion blot out my transgressions.

Psalm 51:1

Not only does he not condemn us; he even brings blessings from the ashes of our failures.

Gini Andrews

PASSAGE FOR THE DAY:
Psalm 51:1–19

For the sake of your word and according to your will, you have done this great thing and made it known to your servant.

2 Samuel 7:21

Lord, I'm glad it is not my responsibility to decide whether or not Christian women should have jobs outside their homes. You've made each of us unique. We have individual abilities, interests and financial circumstances. Thank you that you promise to guide us in making decisions about working. Show us where you want to use us, and stand beside us, Lord.

Marlene Obie

PASSAGE FOR THE DAY:
2 Samuel 7:18–29

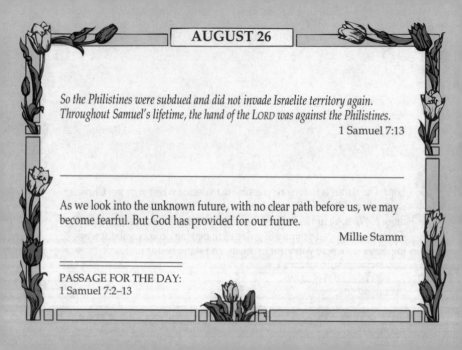

AUGUST 26

So the Philistines were subdued and did not invade Israelite territory again. Throughout Samuel's lifetime, the hand of the LORD was against the Philistines.

1 Samuel 7:13

As we look into the unknown future, with no clear path before us, we may become fearful. But God has provided for our future.

Millie Stamm

PASSAGE FOR THE DAY:
1 Samuel 7:2–13

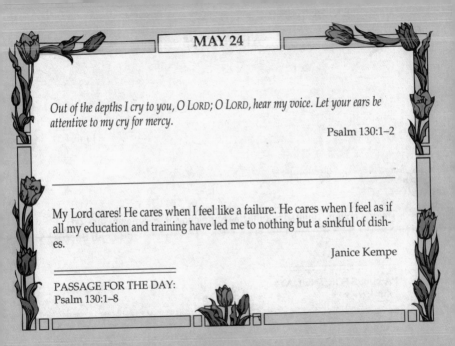

Out of the depths I cry to you, O LORD; O LORD, hear my voice. Let your ears be attentive to my cry for mercy.

Psalm 130:1–2

My Lord cares! He cares when I feel like a failure. He cares when I feel as if all my education and training have led me to nothing but a sinkful of dishes.

Janice Kempe

PASSAGE FOR THE DAY:
Psalm 130:1–8

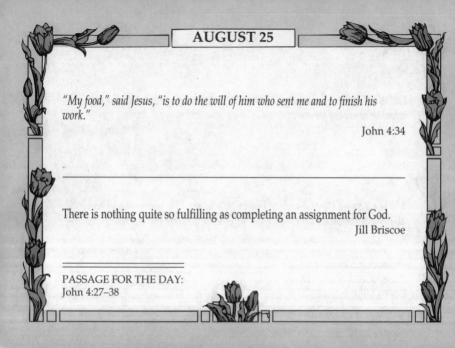

"My food," said Jesus, "is to do the will of him who sent me and to finish his work."

John 4:34

There is nothing quite so fulfilling as completing an assignment for God.

Jill Briscoe

PASSAGE FOR THE DAY:
John 4:27–38

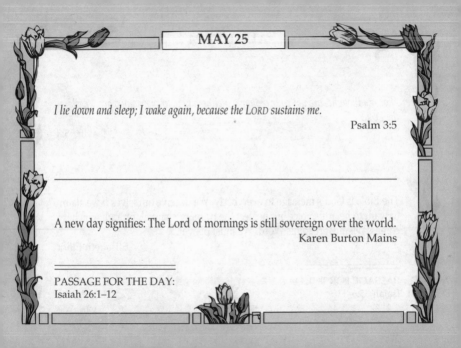

MAY 25

I lie down and sleep; I wake again, because the LORD sustains me.

Psalm 3:5

A new day signifies: The Lord of mornings is still sovereign over the world.

Karen Burton Mains

PASSAGE FOR THE DAY:
Isaiah 26:1–12

AUGUST 24

"For my thoughts are not your thoughts, neither are your ways my ways," declares the LORD.

Isaiah 55:8

The Bible is God's message to everybody. We deceive ourselves if we claim to want to hear his voice but neglect the primary channel through which it comes. We must read his Word. We must obey it.

Elisabeth Elliot

PASSAGE FOR THE DAY:
Isaiah 55:6–11

Endure hardship as discipline; God is treating you as sons. For what son is not disciplined by his father?

Hebrews 12:7

The next time those rough winds sweep through our homes—let's rejoice! It won't be long until we can lift our hearts and laugh in his sunshine . . . in his holiness.

Diane Noble

PASSAGE FOR THE DAY:
Hebrews 12:1–13

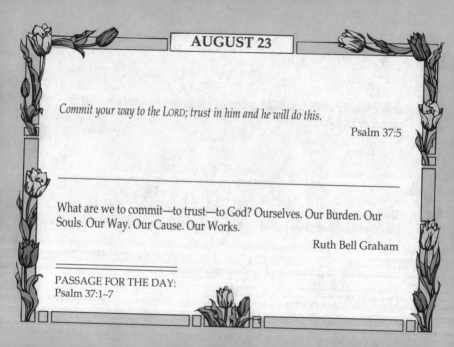

AUGUST 23

Commit your way to the LORD; trust in him and he will do this.

Psalm 37:5

What are we to commit—to trust—to God? Ourselves. Our Burden. Our Souls. Our Way. Our Cause. Our Works.

Ruth Bell Graham

PASSAGE FOR THE DAY:
Psalm 37:1–7

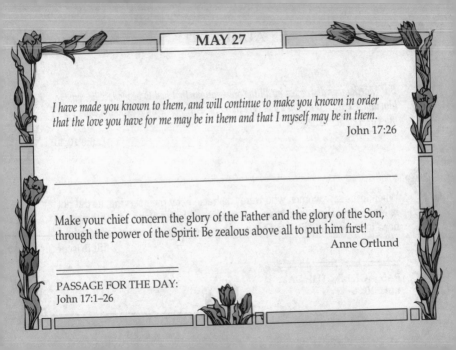

MAY 27

I have made you known to them, and will continue to make you known in order that the love you have for me may be in them and that I myself may be in them.

John 17:26

Make your chief concern the glory of the Father and the glory of the Son, through the power of the Spirit. Be zealous above all to put him first!

Anne Ortlund

PASSAGE FOR THE DAY:
John 17:1–26

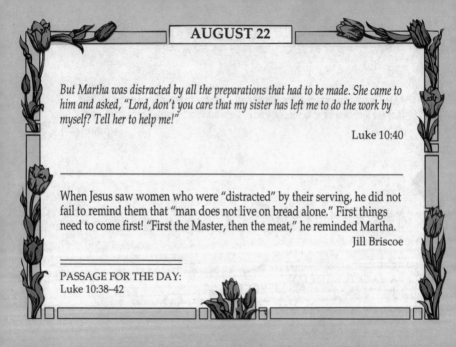

But Martha was distracted by all the preparations that had to be made. She came to him and asked, "Lord, don't you care that my sister has left me to do the work by myself? Tell her to help me!"

Luke 10:40

When Jesus saw women who were "distracted" by their serving, he did not fail to remind them that "man does not live on bread alone." First things need to come first! "First the Master, then the meat," he reminded Martha.

Jill Briscoe

PASSAGE FOR THE DAY:
Luke 10:38–42

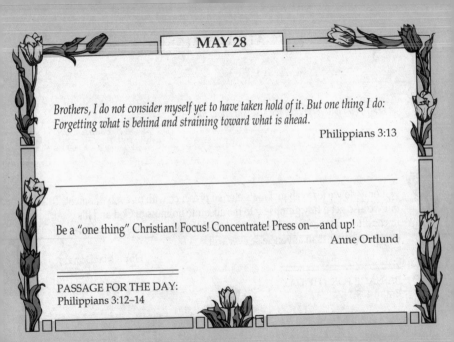

Brothers, I do not consider myself yet to have taken hold of it. But one thing I do: Forgetting what is behind and straining toward what is ahead.

Philippians 3:13

Be a "one thing" Christian! Focus! Concentrate! Press on—and up!

Anne Ortlund

PASSAGE FOR THE DAY:
Philippians 3:12–14

AUGUST 21

O LORD, you have searched me and you know me.

Psalm 139:1

Not only do we learn about God's eternal presence with us every moment, but we also get a tiny glimpse into the absolute holiness of God and his unconditional love for us. We are reminded that God knows and understands us better than anyone else ever will.

Hope MacDonald

PASSAGE FOR THE DAY:
Psalm 139:1–24

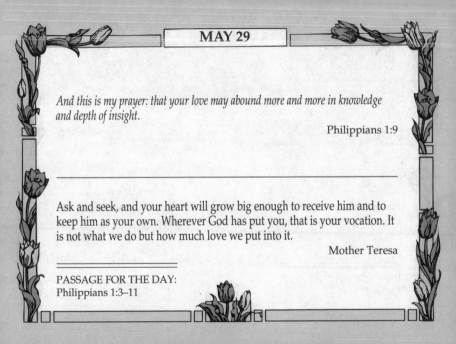

MAY 29

And this is my prayer: that your love may abound more and more in knowledge and depth of insight.

Philippians 1:9

Ask and seek, and your heart will grow big enough to receive him and to keep him as your own. Wherever God has put you, that is your vocation. It is not what we do but how much love we put into it.

Mother Teresa

PASSAGE FOR THE DAY:
Philippians 1:3–11

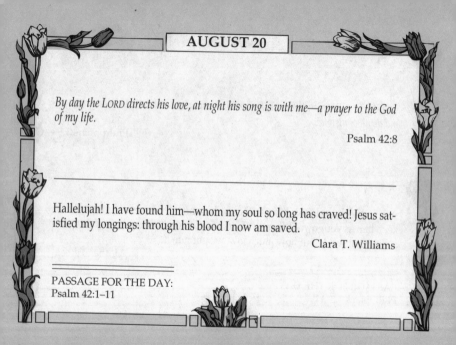

By day the LORD directs his love, at night his song is with me—a prayer to the God of my life.

Psalm 42:8

Hallelujah! I have found him—whom my soul so long has craved! Jesus satisfied my longings: through his blood I now am saved.

Clara T. Williams

PASSAGE FOR THE DAY:
Psalm 42:1–11

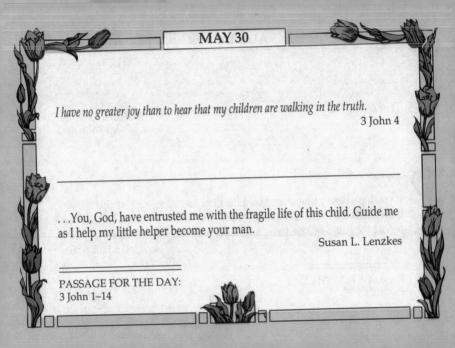

I have no greater joy than to hear that my children are walking in the truth.

3 John 4

...You, God, have entrusted me with the fragile life of this child. Guide me as I help my little helper become your man.

Susan L. Lenzkes

PASSAGE FOR THE DAY:
3 John 1–14

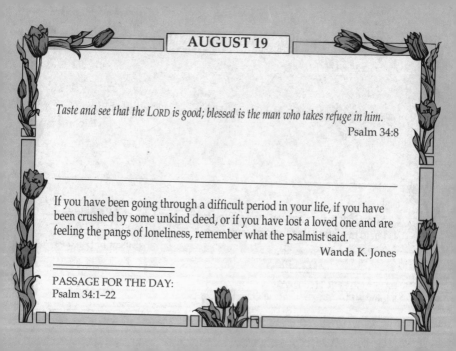

AUGUST 19

Taste and see that the LORD is good; blessed is the man who takes refuge in him.

Psalm 34:8

If you have been going through a difficult period in your life, if you have been crushed by some unkind deed, or if you have lost a loved one and are feeling the pangs of loneliness, remember what the psalmist said.

Wanda K. Jones

PASSAGE FOR THE DAY:
Psalm 34:1–22

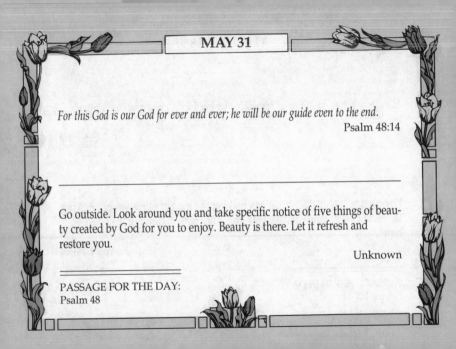

For this God is our God for ever and ever; he will be our guide even to the end.

Psalm 48:14

Go outside. Look around you and take specific notice of five things of beauty created by God for you to enjoy. Beauty is there. Let it refresh and restore you.

Unknown

PASSAGE FOR THE DAY:
Psalm 48

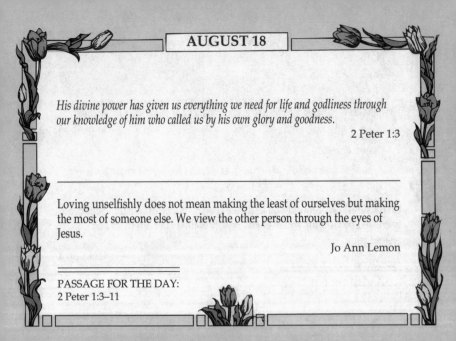

AUGUST 18

His divine power has given us everything we need for life and godliness through our knowledge of him who called us by his own glory and goodness.

2 Peter 1:3

Loving unselfishly does not mean making the least of ourselves but making the most of someone else. We view the other person through the eyes of Jesus.

Jo Ann Lemon

PASSAGE FOR THE DAY:
2 Peter 1:3–11

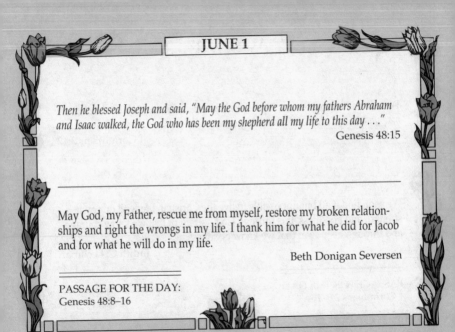

JUNE 1

Then he blessed Joseph and said, "May the God before whom my fathers Abraham and Isaac walked, the God who has been my shepherd all my life to this day . . ."

Genesis 48:15

May God, my Father, rescue me from myself, restore my broken relationships and right the wrongs in my life. I thank him for what he did for Jacob and for what he will do in my life.

Beth Donigan Seversen

PASSAGE FOR THE DAY:
Genesis 48:8–16

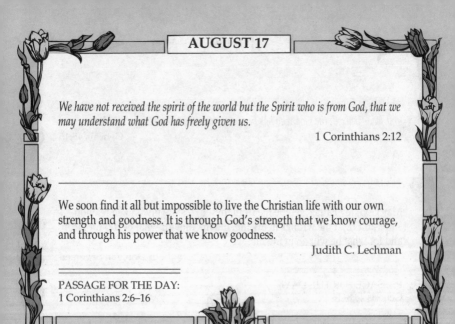

AUGUST 17

We have not received the spirit of the world but the Spirit who is from God, that we may understand what God has freely given us.

1 Corinthians 2:12

We soon find it all but impossible to live the Christian life with our own strength and goodness. It is through God's strength that we know courage, and through his power that we know goodness.

Judith C. Lechman

PASSAGE FOR THE DAY:
1 Corinthians 2:6–16

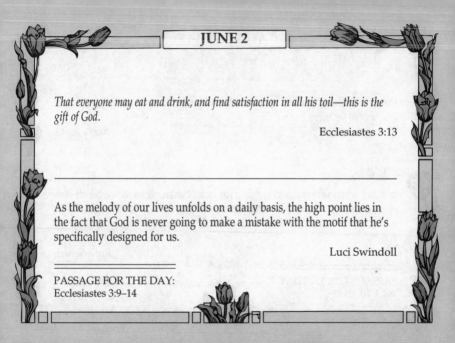

JUNE 2

That everyone may eat and drink, and find satisfaction in all his toil—this is the gift of God.

Ecclesiastes 3:13

As the melody of our lives unfolds on a daily basis, the high point lies in the fact that God is never going to make a mistake with the motif that he's specifically designed for us.

Luci Swindoll

PASSAGE FOR THE DAY:
Ecclesiastes 3:9–14

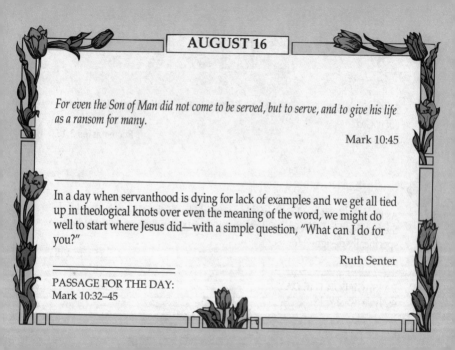

AUGUST 16

For even the Son of Man did not come to be served, but to serve, and to give his life as a ransom for many.

Mark 10:45

In a day when servanthood is dying for lack of examples and we get all tied up in theological knots over even the meaning of the word, we might do well to start where Jesus did—with a simple question, "What can I do for you?"

Ruth Senter

PASSAGE FOR THE DAY:
Mark 10:32–45

Who of you by worrying can add a single hour to his life?

Matthew 6:27

I am ashamed of my worries. Please forgive me and help me to trust you.

Beth Donigan Seversen

PASSAGE FOR THE DAY:
Matthew 6:25–34

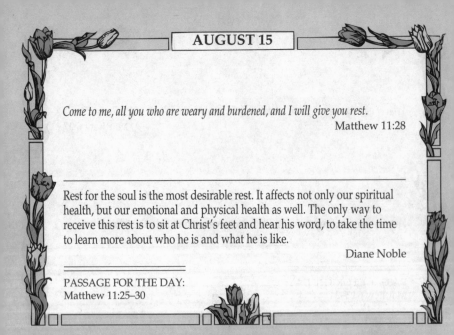

Come to me, all you who are weary and burdened, and I will give you rest.

Matthew 11:28

Rest for the soul is the most desirable rest. It affects not only our spiritual health, but our emotional and physical health as well. The only way to receive this rest is to sit at Christ's feet and hear his word, to take the time to learn more about who he is and what he is like.

Diane Noble

PASSAGE FOR THE DAY:
Matthew 11:25–30

JUNE 4

But as soon as they were at rest, they again did what was evil in your sight. Then you abandoned them to the hand of their enemies so that they ruled over them. And when they cried out to you again, you heard from heaven, and in your compassion you delivered them time after time.

Nehemiah 9:28

A person needs three attitudes to use a time of rest profitably: gratitude for previous blessings, a desire to correct past mistakes and prevent them in the future, and a willingness to occupy himself constructively. The best way to prevent evil is by doing good. Good intentions by themselves are not sufficient to guarantee beneficial rest.

Gien Karssen

PASSAGE FOR THE DAY:
Nehemiah 9:28–37

AUGUST 14

Therefore, I urge you, brothers, in view of God's mercy, to offer your bodies as living sacrifices, holy and pleasing to God—this is your spiritual act of worship. Do not conform any longer to the pattern of this world, but be transformed by the renewing of your mind. Then you will be able to test and approve what God's will is—his good, pleasing and perfect will.

Romans 12:1–2

When we conform to the world's patterns and methods, we do not please God, no matter how good we feel about ourselves or how much other people approve of us. But we do please God when our minds are renewed.

Marie Chapian

PASSAGE FOR THE DAY:
Romans 12:1–8

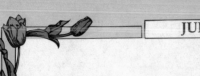

JUNE 5

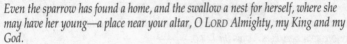

Even the sparrow has found a home, and the swallow a nest for herself, where she may have her young—a place near your altar, O LORD Almighty, my King and my God.

Psalm 84:3

I took out my journal to record some thoughts about this "nest" where I could lay down my own young: 1. A nest is a place of security, rest and provision. 2. It is a place to lay my children on God's altar daily. 3. It will take a sacrifice of time to seek knowledge and wisdom for my young.

Debby Boone

PASSAGE FOR THE DAY:
Psalm 84:1–12

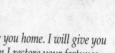

AUGUST 13

"At that time I will gather you; at that time I will bring you home. I will give you honor and praise among all the peoples of the earth when I restore your fortunes before your very eyes," says the LORD.

Zephaniah 3:20

If there is such joy when we return to our earthly homes, imagine the joy of reaching our heavenly home!

Ingrid Trobisch

PASSAGE FOR THE DAY:
Zephaniah 3:14–20

JUNE 6

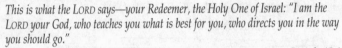

This is what the LORD says—your Redeemer, the Holy One of Israel: "I am the LORD your God, who teaches you what is best for you, who directs you in the way you should go."

Isaiah 48:17

I am grateful, God, that I have finally come to realize your purpose for me. Maybe because life is so filled with defeat and heartbreak, we find ourselves turning to you, yielding ourselves to your will, fighting furiously for selfish, often empty goals. And when this happens we find that you have turned our sufferings and our failures into little stepping-stones.

Marjorie Holmes

PASSAGE FOR THE DAY:
Isaiah 48:12–19

AUGUST 12

Come, O house of Jacob, let us walk in the light of the LORD.

Isaiah 2:5

Lord, help me to learn
I won't be receiving
a miraculous sign
wrought through believing;
when each day I can see
and yet don't apply
Your messages looking me
straight in the eye.

Susan L. Lenzkes

PASSAGE FOR THE DAY:
Isaiah 2:3–5

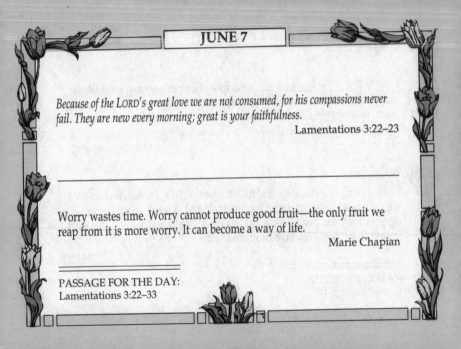

Because of the LORD's great love we are not consumed, for his compassions never fail. They are new every morning; great is your faithfulness.

Lamentations 3:22–23

Worry wastes time. Worry cannot produce good fruit—the only fruit we reap from it is more worry. It can become a way of life.

Marie Chapian

PASSAGE FOR THE DAY:
Lamentations 3:22–33

AUGUST 11

Love the LORD your God with all your heart and with all
your soul and with all your strength. These commandments that I give you today are to be upon your
hearts. Impress them on your children. Talk about them when you sit at home and
when you walk along the road, when you lie down and when you get up.

Deuteronomy 6:5–7

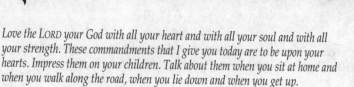

I took a piece of living clay, and gently pressed it day by day, and molded
with my power and art a young child's soft and yielding heart. I came
again when years had gone: It was a man I looked upon. He still that early
impress bore, and I could fashion it no more!

Unknown

PASSAGE FOR THE DAY:
Deuteronomy 6:4–9

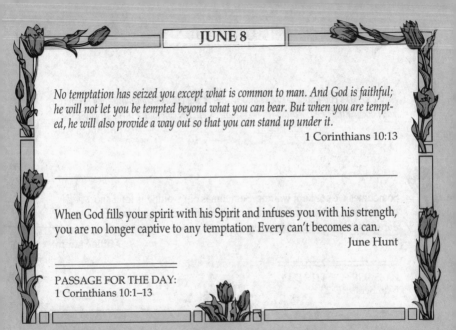

JUNE 8

No temptation has seized you except what is common to man. And God is faithful; he will not let you be tempted beyond what you can bear. But when you are tempted, he will also provide a way out so that you can stand up under it.

1 Corinthians 10:13

When God fills your spirit with his Spirit and infuses you with his strength, you are no longer captive to any temptation. Every can't becomes a can.

June Hunt

PASSAGE FOR THE DAY:
1 Corinthians 10:1–13

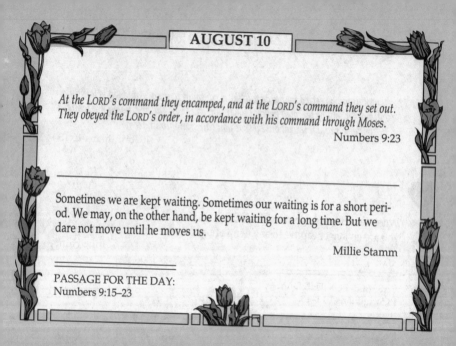

AUGUST 10

At the LORD's command they encamped, and at the LORD's command they set out.
They obeyed the LORD's order, in accordance with his command through Moses.

Numbers 9:23

Sometimes we are kept waiting. Sometimes our waiting is for a short period. We may, on the other hand, be kept waiting for a long time. But we dare not move until he moves us.

Millie Stamm

PASSAGE FOR THE DAY:
Numbers 9:15–23

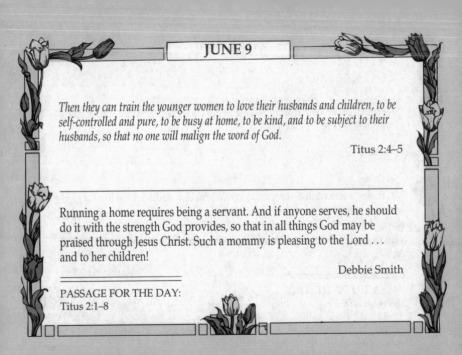

JUNE 9

Then they can train the younger women to love their husbands and children, to be self-controlled and pure, to be busy at home, to be kind, and to be subject to their husbands, so that no one will malign the word of God.

Titus 2:4–5

Running a home requires being a servant. And if anyone serves, he should do it with the strength God provides, so that in all things God may be praised through Jesus Christ. Such a mommy is pleasing to the Lord . . . and to her children!

Debbie Smith

PASSAGE FOR THE DAY:
Titus 2:1–8

AUGUST 9

But encourage one another daily, as long as it is called Today, so that none of you may be hardened by sin's deceitfulness.

Hebrews 3:13

Mr. Barns, a retired and somewhat senile bachelor, radiated the love of God and was loved by the people of the church. "God has blessed many people through your hands," he said. I have often thought about that humble servant of God, willing to go out of his way to encourage a tired young mother.

Kathryn Hillen

PASSAGE FOR THE DAY:
Hebrews 3:12–19

For everyone born of God overcomes the world. This is the victory that has overcome the world, even our faith.

1 John 5:4

By faith you've already overcome the world. When God commissions, he empowers. That power is absolutely yours, by faith. Take it and head out. The victories are just beginning.

Luci Swindoll

PASSAGE FOR THE DAY:
1 John 5:1–12

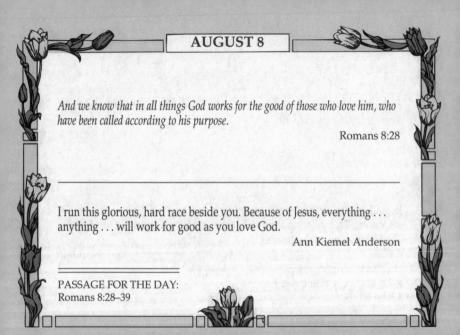

AUGUST 8

And we know that in all things God works for the good of those who love him, who have been called according to his purpose.

Romans 8:28

I run this glorious, hard race beside you. Because of Jesus, everything . . . anything . . . will work for good as you love God.

Ann Kiemel Anderson

PASSAGE FOR THE DAY:
Romans 8:28–39

I have been crucified with Christ and I no longer live, but Christ lives in me. The life I live in the body, I live by faith in the Son of God, who loved me and gave himself for me.

Galatians 2:20

Christianity isn't a narcotic that dulls you into obedience. It involves battle—it's excruciating to give up control. But that is why we must not feel despair if we are struggling. To struggle does not mean we are incorrigible. It means we are alive!

Rebecca Manley Pippert

PASSAGE FOR THE DAY:
Galatians 2:15–21

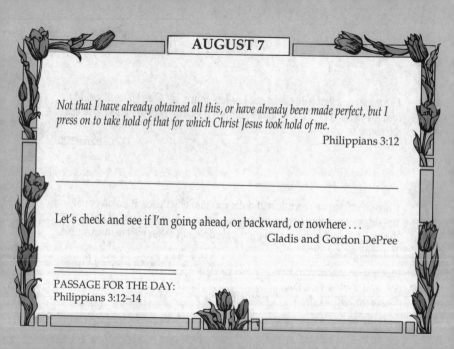

AUGUST 7

Not that I have already obtained all this, or have already been made perfect, but I press on to take hold of that for which Christ Jesus took hold of me.

Philippians 3:12

Let's check and see if I'm going ahead, or backward, or nowhere . . .

Gladis and Gordon DePree

PASSAGE FOR THE DAY:
Philippians 3:12–14

JUNE 12

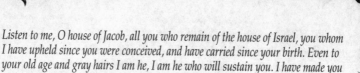

Listen to me, O house of Jacob, all you who remain of the house of Israel, you whom I have upheld since you were conceived, and have carried since your birth. Even to your old age and gray hairs I am he, I am he who will sustain you. I have made you and I will carry you; I will sustain you and I will rescue you.

Isaiah 46:3–4

We're on a pilgrim road. It's rough and steep, and it winds uphill to the very end. We can lift up our eyes and see the unseen: a celestial city, a light, a welcome and an ineffable face. We shall behold him. We shall be like him. And that makes a difference in how we go about aging.

Elisabeth Elliot

PASSAGE FOR THE DAY:
Isaiah 46:1–13

AUGUST 6

He cuts off every branch in me that bears no fruit, while every branch that does bear fruit he prunes so that it will be even more fruitful.

John 15:2

We need God's help even to desire to yield ourselves to his pruning. May God bring people and events into our lives that will sanctify us so that we might bear true spiritual fruit for his glory and his kingdom's sake.

Carol L. Baldwin

PASSAGE FOR THE DAY:
John 15:1–6

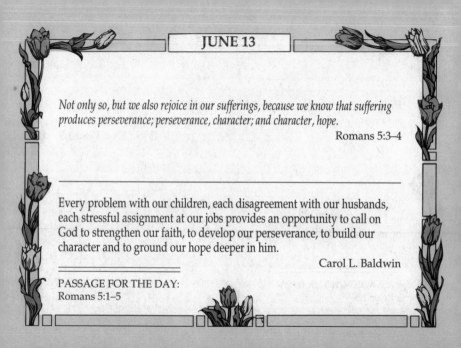

JUNE 13

Not only so, but we also rejoice in our sufferings, because we know that suffering produces perseverance; perseverance, character; and character, hope.

Romans 5:3–4

Every problem with our children, each disagreement with our husbands, each stressful assignment at our jobs provides an opportunity to call on God to strengthen our faith, to develop our perseverance, to build our character and to ground our hope deeper in him.

Carol L. Baldwin

PASSAGE FOR THE DAY:
Romans 5:1–5

AUGUST 5

His divine power has given us everything we need for life and godliness through our knowledge of him who called us by his own glory and goodness.

2 Peter 1:3

We can't—by our own power—change our lives. When we open the door and allow God's life-changing power to enter in . . . step by step, moment by moment . . . he begins a good work in us.

Diane Noble

PASSAGE FOR THE DAY:
2 Peter 1:3–9

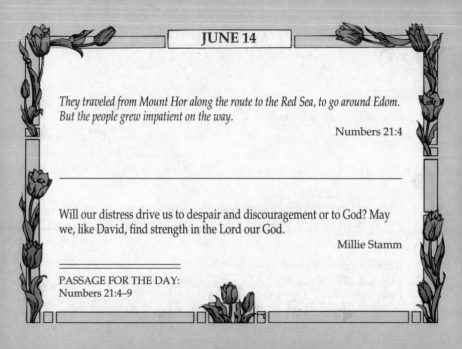

They traveled from Mount Hor along the route to the Red Sea, to go around Edom. But the people grew impatient on the way.

Numbers 21:4

Will our distress drive us to despair and discouragement or to God? May we, like David, find strength in the Lord our God.

Millie Stamm

PASSAGE FOR THE DAY:
Numbers 21:4–9

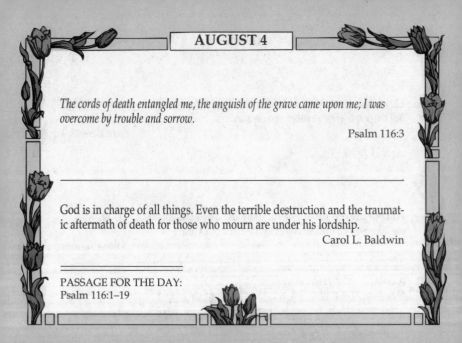

AUGUST 4

The cords of death entangled me, the anguish of the grave came upon me; I was overcome by trouble and sorrow.

Psalm 116:3

God is in charge of all things. Even the terrible destruction and the traumatic aftermath of death for those who mourn are under his lordship.

Carol L. Baldwin

PASSAGE FOR THE DAY:
Psalm 116:1–19

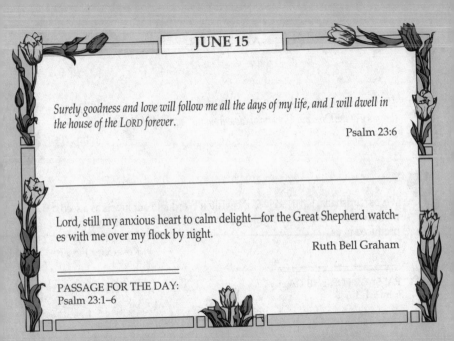

JUNE 15

Surely goodness and love will follow me all the days of my life, and I will dwell in the house of the LORD forever.

Psalm 23:6

Lord, still my anxious heart to calm delight—for the Great Shepherd watches with me over my flock by night.

Ruth Bell Graham

PASSAGE FOR THE DAY:
Psalm 23:1–6

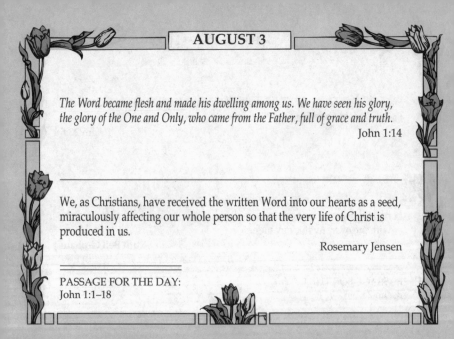

AUGUST 3

The Word became flesh and made his dwelling among us. We have seen his glory, the glory of the One and Only, who came from the Father, full of grace and truth.

John 1:14

We, as Christians, have received the written Word into our hearts as a seed, miraculously affecting our whole person so that the very life of Christ is produced in us.

Rosemary Jensen

PASSAGE FOR THE DAY:
John 1:1–18

JUNE 16

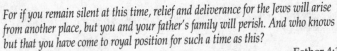

For if you remain silent at this time, relief and deliverance for the Jews will arise from another place, but you and your father's family will perish. And who knows but that you have come to royal position for such a time as this?

Esther 4:14

Esther had her opportunity; we have ours. A difficult and dangerous human task is no excuse for failing to perform divinely assigned duty. God chooses where we are called to serve; we choose, as did Esther, whether or not to respond in obedience to that call.

Dorothy Patterson

PASSAGE FOR THE DAY:
Esther 3:13–4:17

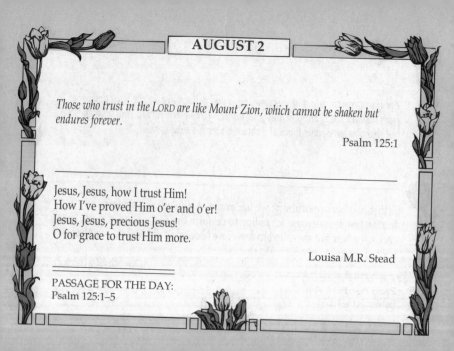

AUGUST 2

*Those who trust in the LORD are like Mount Zion, which cannot be shaken but
endures forever.*

Psalm 125:1

Jesus, Jesus, how I trust Him!
How I've proved Him o'er and o'er!
Jesus, Jesus, precious Jesus!
O for grace to trust Him more.

Louisa M.R. Stead

PASSAGE FOR THE DAY:
Psalm 125:1–5

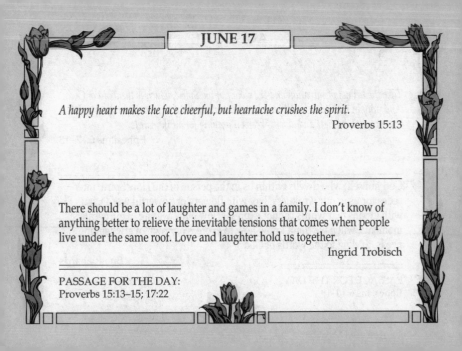

JUNE 17

A happy heart makes the face cheerful, but heartache crushes the spirit.

Proverbs 15:13

There should be a lot of laughter and games in a family. I don't know of anything better to relieve the inevitable tensions that comes when people live under the same roof. Love and laughter hold us together.

Ingrid Trobisch

PASSAGE FOR THE DAY:
Proverbs 15:13–15; 17:22

AUGUST 1

Take the helmet of salvation and the sword of the Spirit, which is the word of God. And pray in the Spirit on all occasions with all kinds of prayers and requests. With this in mind, be alert and always keep on praying for all the saints.

Ephesians 6:17–18

God himself, who dwells within us in the person of the Holy Spirit, intercedes for us in our weakness. Not with flowery or powerful words, but with groans that words cannot express. How empowering in our weakest moments, when we don't know how to express our own overwhelming needs, to cling to the words of God.

Sue Richards

PASSAGE FOR THE DAY:
Ephesians 6:10–18

Ah, Sovereign LORD, you have made the heavens and the earth by your great power and outstretched arm. Nothing is too hard for you.

Jeremiah 32:17

Our God hasn't changed. The God of creation is the same yesterday, today, and forever. His power hasn't diminished.

Diane Noble

PASSAGE FOR THE DAY:
Jeremiah 32:16–29

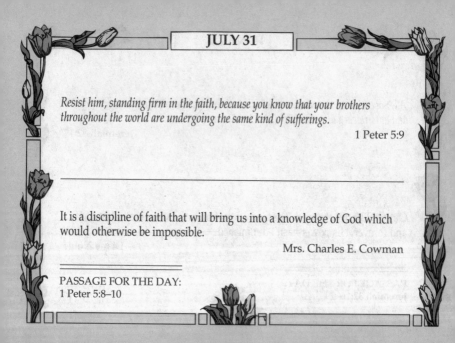

Resist him, standing firm in the faith, because you know that your brothers throughout the world are undergoing the same kind of sufferings.

1 Peter 5:9

It is a discipline of faith that will bring us into a knowledge of God which would otherwise be impossible.

Mrs. Charles E. Cowman

PASSAGE FOR THE DAY:
1 Peter 5:8–10

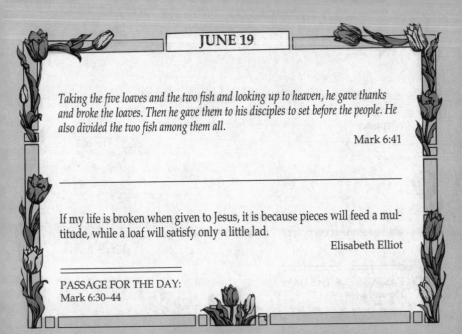

JUNE 19

Taking the five loaves and the two fish and looking up to heaven, he gave thanks and broke the loaves. Then he gave them to his disciples to set before the people. He also divided the two fish among them all.

Mark 6:41

If my life is broken when given to Jesus, it is because pieces will feed a multitude, while a loaf will satisfy only a little lad.

Elisabeth Elliot

PASSAGE FOR THE DAY:
Mark 6:30–44

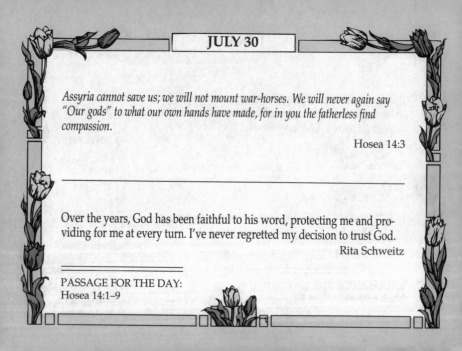

Assyria cannot save us; we will not mount war-horses. We will never again say "Our gods" to what our own hands have made, for in you the fatherless find compassion.

Hosea 14:3

Over the years, God has been faithful to his word, protecting me and providing for me at every turn. I've never regretted my decision to trust God.

Rita Schweitz

PASSAGE FOR THE DAY:
Hosea 14:1–9

I do not understand what I do. For what I want to do I do not do, but what I hate I do.

Romans 7:15

To allow ourselves to be trapped in Satan's snare—wallowing in despair—is to disparage the limitless, liberating grace of God.

Jeanette Lockerbie

PASSAGE FOR THE DAY:
Romans 7:14–21

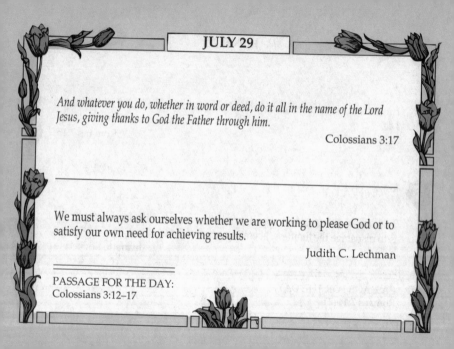

And whatever you do, whether in word or deed, do it all in the name of the Lord Jesus, giving thanks to God the Father through him.

Colossians 3:17

We must always ask ourselves whether we are working to please God or to satisfy our own need for achieving results.

Judith C. Lechman

PASSAGE FOR THE DAY:
Colossians 3:12–17

Has not the LORD made them one? In flesh and spirit they are his. And why one? Because he was seeking godly offspring. So guard yourself in your spirit, and do not break faith with the wife of your youth.

Malachi 2:15

We must use the Word of God as our basis for sorting out right from wrong, the basis for making decisions or resolving conflicts.

Beverly LaHaye

PASSAGE FOR THE DAY:
Malachi 2:13–16

What do you prefer? Shall I come to you with a whip, or in love and with a gentle spirit?

1 Corinthians 4:21

Grace gives without the receiver realizing how great the gift really is.

Rebecca Manley Pippert

PASSAGE FOR THE DAY:
1 Corinthians 4:14–21

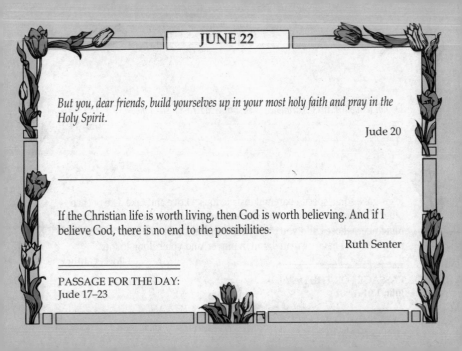

JUNE 22

But you, dear friends, build yourselves up in your most holy faith and pray in the Holy Spirit.

Jude 20

If the Christian life is worth living, then God is worth believing. And if I believe God, there is no end to the possibilities.

Ruth Senter

PASSAGE FOR THE DAY:
Jude 17–23

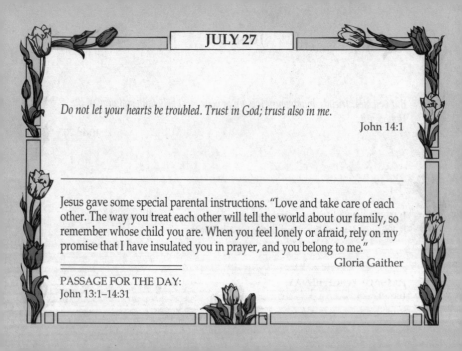

JULY 27

Do not let your hearts be troubled. Trust in God; trust also in me.

John 14:1

Jesus gave some special parental instructions. "Love and take care of each other. The way you treat each other will tell the world about our family, so remember whose child you are. When you feel lonely or afraid, rely on my promise that I have insulated you in prayer, and you belong to me."

Gloria Gaither

PASSAGE FOR THE DAY:
John 13:1–14:31

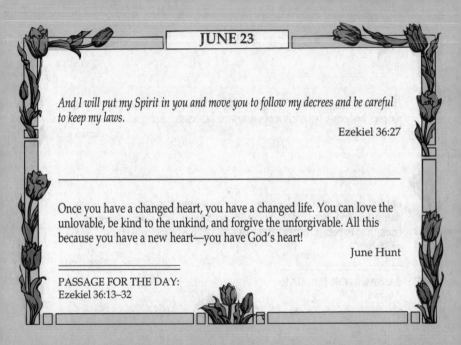

JUNE 23

And I will put my Spirit in you and move you to follow my decrees and be careful to keep my laws.

Ezekiel 36:27

Once you have a changed heart, you have a changed life. You can love the unlovable, be kind to the unkind, and forgive the unforgivable. All this because you have a new heart—you have God's heart!

June Hunt

PASSAGE FOR THE DAY:
Ezekiel 36:13–32

Hear this word, you cows of Bashan on Mount Samaria, you women who oppress the poor and crush the needy and say to your husbands, "Bring us some drinks!"

Amos 4:1

I'm certainly a privileged woman in today's American society. I'm often pampered and indulged. But may I never become selfish or self-centered enough to expect it or think it my due. May I never resemble those "cows of Bashan"!

Jean E. Syswerda

PASSAGE FOR THE DAY:
Amos 4:1–5

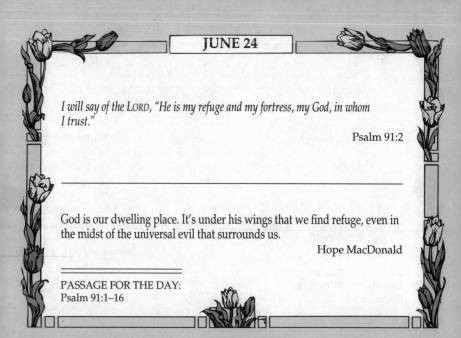

JUNE 24

I will say of the Lord, *"He is my refuge and my fortress, my God, in whom I trust."*

Psalm 91:2

God is our dwelling place. It's under his wings that we find refuge, even in the midst of the universal evil that surrounds us.

Hope MacDonald

PASSAGE FOR THE DAY:
Psalm 91:1–16

By day the LORD directs his love, at night his song is with me—a prayer to the God of my life.

Psalm 42:8

To become a candidate for his comfort, you first must open yourself up to the pain of mourning.

Maureen Rank

PASSAGE FOR THE DAY:
Psalm 42:1–8

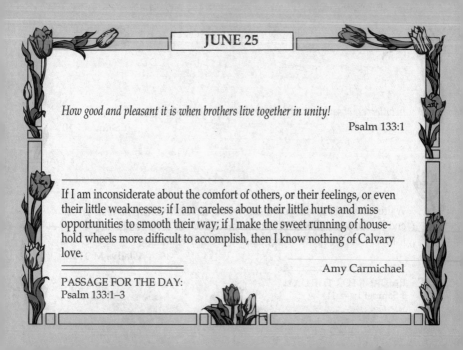

JUNE 25

How good and pleasant it is when brothers live together in unity!

Psalm 133:1

If I am inconsiderate about the comfort of others, or their feelings, or even their little weaknesses; if I am careless about their little hurts and miss opportunities to smooth their way; if I make the sweet running of household wheels more difficult to accomplish, then I know nothing of Calvary love.

Amy Carmichael

PASSAGE FOR THE DAY:
Psalm 133:1–3

In bitterness of soul Hannah wept much and prayed to the LORD.

1 Samuel 1:10

Waiting is one of the hardest things we do, especially when the years go by and we see no fulfillment of our dreams and hopes. It's a good thing to learn to wait; we spend a large amount of our lives waiting.

Gladys M. Hunt

PASSAGE FOR THE DAY:
1 Samuel 1:1–2:11

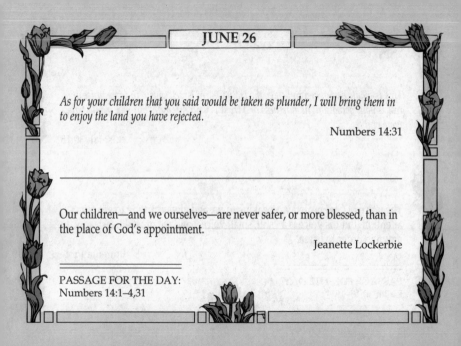

JUNE 26

As for your children that you said would be taken as plunder, I will bring them in to enjoy the land you have rejected.

Numbers 14:31

Our children—and we ourselves—are never safer, or more blessed, than in the place of God's appointment.

Jeanette Lockerbie

PASSAGE FOR THE DAY:
Numbers 14:1–4,31

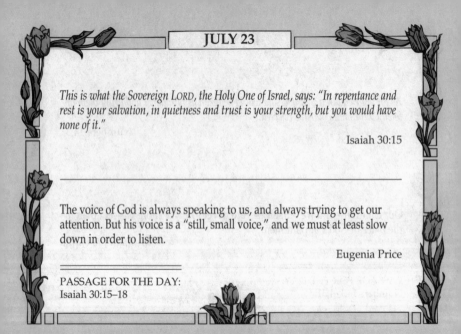

This is what the Sovereign LORD, the Holy One of Israel, says: "In repentance and rest is your salvation, in quietness and trust is your strength, but you would have none of it."

Isaiah 30:15

The voice of God is always speaking to us, and always trying to get our attention. But his voice is a "still, small voice," and we must at least slow down in order to listen.

Eugenia Price

PASSAGE FOR THE DAY:
Isaiah 30:15–18

JUNE 27

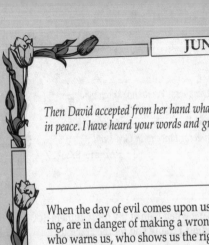

Then David accepted from her hand what she had brought him and said, "Go home in peace. I have heard your words and granted your request."

1 Samuel 25:35

When the day of evil comes upon us, when we, confused by negative thinking, are in danger of making a wrong decision, may we also meet someone who warns us, who shows us the right way, who has our good conscience at heart. That is a gift of peace from God.

Gien Karssen

PASSAGE FOR THE DAY:
1 Samuel 25:4–35

JULY 22

In the same way, the Spirit helps us in our weakness. We do not know what we ought to pray for, but the Spirit himself intercedes for us with groans that words cannot express. And he who searches our heart knows the mind of the Spirit, because the Spirit intercedes for the saints in accordance with God's will.

Romans 8:26–27

Abba, Father, your love and concern for me when I am at my most vulnerable times in life is beyond my understanding. I thank you for the gracious gift of your Holy Spirit. Amen.

Sue Richards

PASSAGE FOR THE DAY:
Romans 8:18–27

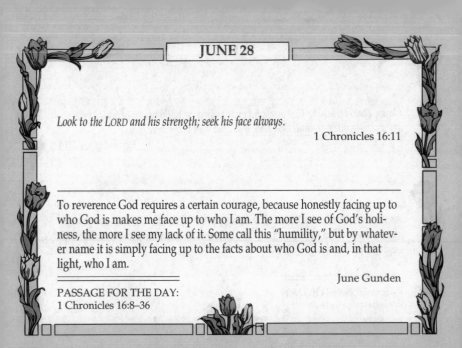

JUNE 28

Look to the Lord and his strength; seek his face always.

1 Chronicles 16:11

To reverence God requires a certain courage, because honestly facing up to who God is makes me face up to who I am. The more I see of God's holiness, the more I see my lack of it. Some call this "humility," but by whatever name it is simply facing up to the facts about who God is and, in that light, who I am.

June Gunden

PASSAGE FOR THE DAY:
1 Chronicles 16:8–36

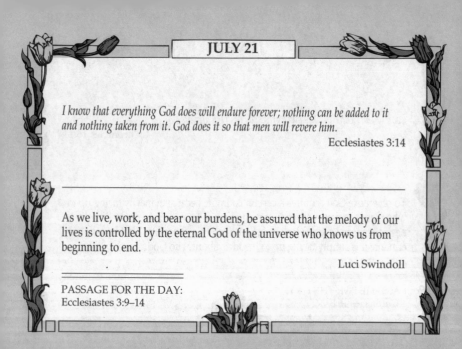

JULY 21

I know that everything God does will endure forever; nothing can be added to it and nothing taken from it. God does it so that men will revere him.

Ecclesiastes 3:14

As we live, work, and bear our burdens, be assured that the melody of our lives is controlled by the eternal God of the universe who knows us from beginning to end.

Luci Swindoll

PASSAGE FOR THE DAY:
Ecclesiastes 3:9–14

Fear the LORD your God and serve him. Hold fast to him and take your oaths in his name.

Deuteronomy 10:20

Each time life throws us a punch, we can do a deep-knee bend, forcing our muscles of faith, hope, and understanding to stretch.... All of this requires considerable daily "give." Such give is not a one-time choice but a lifetime of generosity, spontaneity, and openness to truth.

Susan L. Lenzkes

PASSAGE FOR THE DAY:
Deuteronomy 10:12-22

JULY 20

Is any one of you in trouble? He should pray. Is anyone happy? Let him sing songs of praise.

James 5:13

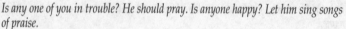

Pray to Jesus, our risen Lord, from the child in your heart. Here are four subjects to guide you: 1. Jesus is here. 2. Thank you, Lord. 3. Forgive me, Lord. 4. Help my sister/brother.

Rosalind Rinker

PASSAGE FOR THE DAY:
James 5:13–16

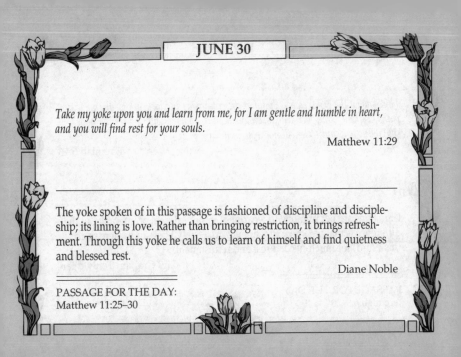

JUNE 30

Take my yoke upon you and learn from me, for I am gentle and humble in heart, and you will find rest for your souls.

Matthew 11:29

The yoke spoken of in this passage is fashioned of discipline and discipleship; its lining is love. Rather than bringing restriction, it brings refreshment. Through this yoke he calls us to learn of himself and find quietness and blessed rest.

Diane Noble

PASSAGE FOR THE DAY:
Matthew 11:25–30

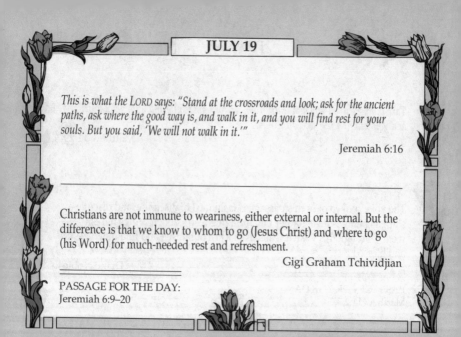

JULY 19

This is what the LORD says: "Stand at the crossroads and look; ask for the ancient paths, ask where the good way is, and walk in it, and you will find rest for your souls. But you said, 'We will not walk in it.'"

Jeremiah 6:16

Christians are not immune to weariness, either external or internal. But the difference is that we know to whom to go (Jesus Christ) and where to go (his Word) for much-needed rest and refreshment.

Gigi Graham Tchividjian

PASSAGE FOR THE DAY:
Jeremiah 6:9–20

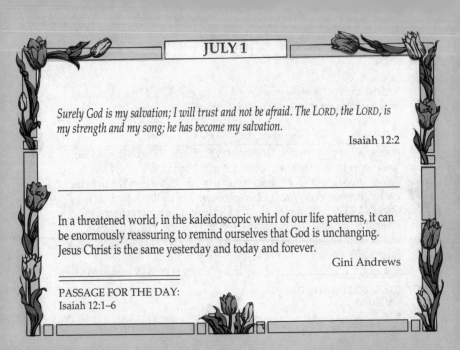

JULY 1

Surely God is my salvation; I will trust and not be afraid. The LORD, the LORD, is my strength and my song; he has become my salvation.

Isaiah 12:2

In a threatened world, in the kaleidoscopic whirl of our life patterns, it can be enormously reassuring to remind ourselves that God is unchanging. Jesus Christ is the same yesterday and today and forever.

Gini Andrews

PASSAGE FOR THE DAY:
Isaiah 12:1–6

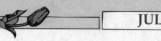

JULY 18

So Satan went out from the presence of the LORD and afflicted Job with painful sores from the soles of his feet to the top of his head.

Job 2:7

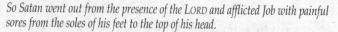

A mole is a spy who works for an enemy and leaks "information" to the "bad" guys in order to hurt, tarnish the reputation of, or destroy the "good" guys. Lately, I have been trying to flush out the enemy's mole in my life. It seems every time I get a specific area of my life submitted to Christ's lordship, the mole leaks that highly sensitive information. For, invariably, it is that area that is attacked by all kinds of temptations or accusations. I am learning to expect the leaks, suspect the moles, and recognize Satan's afflictions.

Beth Donigan Seversen

PASSAGE FOR THE DAY:
Job 2:1–10

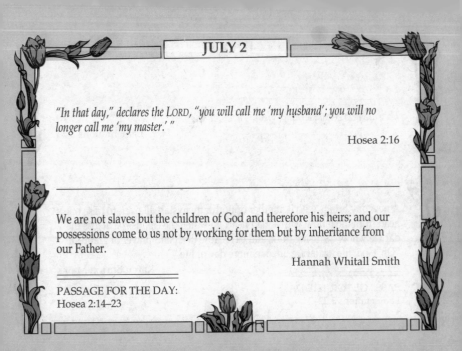

"In that day," declares the LORD, *"you will call me 'my husband'; you will no longer call me 'my master.'"*

Hosea 2:16

We are not slaves but the children of God and therefore his heirs; and our possessions come to us not by working for them but by inheritance from our Father.

Hannah Whitall Smith

PASSAGE FOR THE DAY:
Hosea 2:14–23

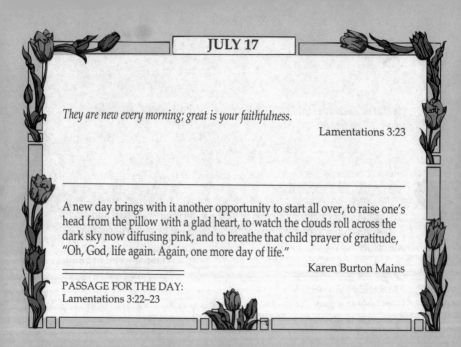

JULY 17

They are new every morning; great is your faithfulness.

Lamentations 3:23

A new day brings with it another opportunity to start all over, to raise one's head from the pillow with a glad heart, to watch the clouds roll across the dark sky now diffusing pink, and to breathe that child prayer of gratitude, "Oh, God, life again. Again, one more day of life."

Karen Burton Mains

PASSAGE FOR THE DAY:
Lamentations 3:22–23

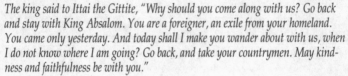

The king said to Ittai the Gittite, "Why should you come along with us? Go back and stay with King Absalom. You are a foreigner, an exile from your homeland. You came only yesterday. And today shall I make you wander about with us, when I do not know where I am going? Go back, and take your countrymen. May kindness and faithfulness be with you."

2 Samuel 15:19–20

David was humiliated, weakened and mocked. Yet in this passage we see the result of David's decision to look away from the terrible circumstances in his life and shift his attention to God.

Myrna Alexander

PASSAGE FOR THE DAY:
2 Samuel 15:13–37

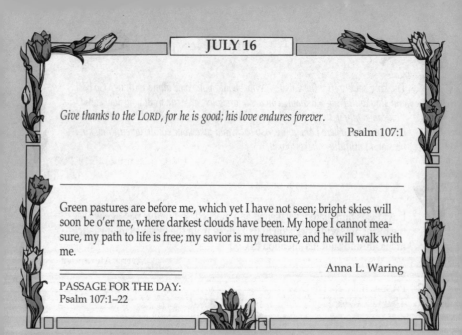

JULY 16

Give thanks to the LORD, for he is good; his love endures forever.

Psalm 107:1

Green pastures are before me, which yet I have not seen; bright skies will soon be o'er me, where darkest clouds have been. My hope I cannot measure, my path to life is free; my savior is my treasure, and he will walk with me.

Anna L. Waring

PASSAGE FOR THE DAY:
Psalm 107:1–22

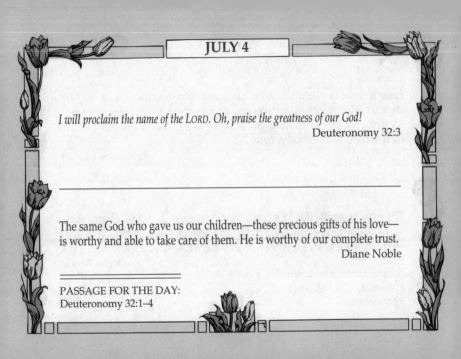

I will proclaim the name of the LORD. Oh, praise the greatness of our God!

Deuteronomy 32:3

The same God who gave us our children—these precious gifts of his love—is worthy and able to take care of them. He is worthy of our complete trust.

Diane Noble

PASSAGE FOR THE DAY:
Deuteronomy 32:1–4

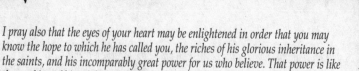

JULY 15

I pray also that the eyes of your heart may be enlightened in order that you may know the hope to which he has called you, the riches of his glorious inheritance in the saints, and his incomparably great power for us who believe. That power is like the working of his mighty strength.

Ephesians 1:18–19

The areas of my life that I feel are barren . . . useless . . . dead . . . burnt-out . . . those are the areas that he will fill with nothing less than himself so that I too can be the fullness of him who fills everything in every way.

Debby Boone

PASSAGE FOR THE DAY:
Ephesians 1:3–23

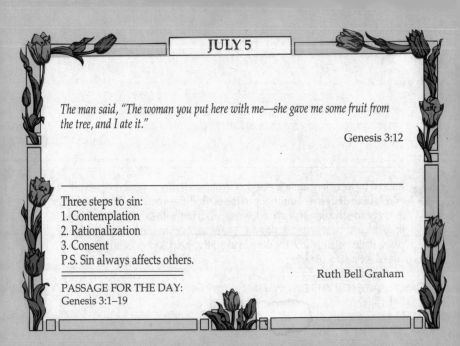

JULY 5

The man said, "The woman you put here with me—she gave me some fruit from the tree, and I ate it."

Genesis 3:12

Three steps to sin:
1. Contemplation
2. Rationalization
3. Consent
P.S. Sin always affects others.

Ruth Bell Graham

PASSAGE FOR THE DAY:
Genesis 3:1–19

And she gave birth to her firstborn, a son. She wrapped him in cloths and placed him in a manger, because there was no room for them in the inn.

Luke 2:7

Enticed by love they came to see God in human frailty, a newborn babe of purest birth delivered, squirming to the earth. This promised child clutched in his hand salvation sent at God's command. But with salvation death was brought, and pain and suffering too, were caught entangled in his tiny palm; flailed silently into the calm of night that held, so innocently, the man who'd set his people free.

Rebekah Tempest

PASSAGE FOR THE DAY:
Luke 2:1–7

JULY 6

So he went down and dipped himself in the Jordan seven times, as the man of God had told him, and his flesh was restored and became clean like that of a young boy.

2 Kings 5:14

The Master will never give us "big" things to do if we have been unwilling to do "small" things.

June Gunden

PASSAGE FOR THE DAY:
2 Kings 5:1–15

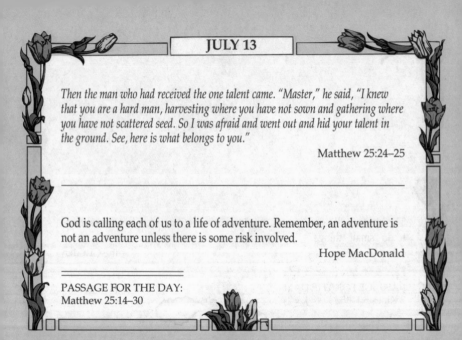

JULY 13

Then the man who had received the one talent came. "Master," he said, "I knew that you are a hard man, harvesting where you have not sown and gathering where you have not scattered seed. So I was afraid and went out and hid your talent in the ground. See, here is what belongs to you."

Matthew 25:24–25

God is calling each of us to a life of adventure. Remember, an adventure is not an adventure unless there is some risk involved.

Hope MacDonald

PASSAGE FOR THE DAY:
Matthew 25:14–30

JULY 7

I praise you for remembering me in everything and for holding to the teachings, just as I passed them on to you.

1 Corinthians 11:2

A growing emptiness creates a hunger for the Christian principles that once guided us, the fellowship that church involvement provided us, the family devotions that once united us. I believe the Holy Spirit uses our childhood memories to whet our appetite for the things of God. As we obediently search out his will and obey it, we in turn are establishing a Christian tradition for our children.

Alma Barkman

PASSAGE FOR THE DAY:
1 Corinthians 11:2–16

JULY 12

How can I give you up, Ephraim? How can I hand you over, Israel? How can I treat you like Admah? How can I make you like Zeboiim? My heart is changed within me; all my compassion is aroused."

Hosea 11:8

As God showers us with comfort through his Word and through other believers, we in turn are to redirect the stream of his mercy to others. We are not to hoard God's love, but to overflow with the good news of his compassion to all.

Barbara Bush

PASSAGE FOR THE DAY:
Hosea 11:1–11

JULY 8

For it is written: "Be holy, because I am holy."

1 Peter 1:16

___

God calls you holy. With his presence inside you, he will produce the impossible through you.

June Hunt

PASSAGE FOR THE DAY:
1 Peter 1:13–25

JULY 11

Therefore, I urge you, brothers, in view of God's mercy, to offer your bodies as living sacrifices, holy and pleasing to God—this is your spiritual act of worship.

Romans 12:1

If somehow in our imagination we are able to recreate all the qualities of perfect man and perfect woman in one being, we have, perhaps, a faint hint of who God really is. And, as we reflect on who God is, we see a picture of the image we carry in ourselves individually.

Ruth A. Tucker

PASSAGE FOR THE DAY:
Romans 12:1–2